Number 176520

The Story of Paul Argiewicz
A Teenage Holocaust Survivor

Deanne L. Joseph

Preface by Holocaust scholar Kenneth Waltzer, Ph.D.
With additional historical information and documents

2ND EDITION

Number 176520
The Story of Paul Argiewicz
A Teenage Holocaust Survivor

● ● ●

ISBN 13: 978-0-615-30726-8

Please direct all inquiries or requests for permission to use material from this book to: 262-893-5671 • bluethreadinc@yahoo.com

BLUE THREAD, INC.
PO BOX 388
SALEM, WI
53168-0388

For all other inquiries: paulsstory@yahoo.com
(See back of this book for ordering and other information.)

Text and Illustrations Copyright © 2009, Blue Thread Inc.
Printed in the United States of America.

Photography Credits: © YIVO Archives, U.S. Armed Forces, permission of Mr. and Mrs. Paul Argiewicz, Getty Images, Yad Vashem — Israel, St. Xavier University, Mr. Larry Barrett, Congregation B'nai Maccabim

Cover Photograph Credit: Chieferu of IStockPhoto Agency

Cover design, book design, illustrations, photo-retouch, typesetting and charts by M. Hurley, Teknigrammaton Graphics, Inc.
www.teknigram.com • 773-973-5061

Editing and typesetting by Linda Wolf • Network Publishing Partners, Inc.
www.networkpublishingpartners.com • 847-998-1716

Editing by Dana Joseph

Fact-checking by Rachel Williams

A Word to the Reader

The deliberate sanction and dissemination of hatred is a foreign concept to most Americans of the 21st century. In spite of internal historical and enduring social prejudices, we continue to struggle for the emergence of justice and equality for all people. Irrational and vicious hatred, while it still exists in pockets in our nation, is not only an embarrassment, it is the antithesis of the contemporary values most Americans share. From the onset of social awareness in childhood, we are coached in our homes, schools, and religious institutions in the acquisition of skills, attitudes, and education — usually geared at promoting tolerance and acceptance of others. We learn to share, to communicate, to engage. We are taught that the qualities and characteristics that constitute a human being — skin color, sex, religion, cultural heritage, physical attributes — though different from our own, have value. We are taught that human life, regardless of its appearance, is intrinsically precious and that we should endeavor to live in peace with everyone.

Despite the efforts of the majority, however, there are those who hold the fervent conviction that their domain has been infiltrated by individuals, factions, and tribes of a "subhuman" race. Those who view themselves as superior believe the infiltrators to be nature's mistake. With haughty contempt, they proclaim that these "vermin" possess neither rights nor soul, but exist as parasites on Earth, doing little more than consuming precious resources of air, water, food, and space. In the eyes of the racial or religious elitist, these "subhumans" are specimens of evil, rejected by God and, for the welfare of the human race, must be eradicated. They believe that it is incumbent upon those of the "supreme sect" to accomplish their "God-given task." Failure to do so, they contend, will result in their own extinction.

Those who adhere to this way of thinking insist that the "subhumans" are not people. They are not animals. They are lower than animals. They are nothing more than numbers.

This is the story of one such number. ✡

i

Author's Acknowledgements

Paul's story would never have been made into a book had it not been for the beyond-generous contribution of time, energy, and love of several people. Their devotion to this project leaves me in awe. With all of my heart, my most sincere thanks to everyone who gave so selflessly.

Paul and Cheryl Argiewicz — for everything and more . . . there simply are not enough words to tell you how grateful I am that God has granted me the honor of being part of your lives. I love you immensely and will eternally treasure the time we have been given to share on this earth. Thank you for allowing me to be the one to write your story. May you be blessed with long life, and may your years be filled with love, health, joy, and shalom. May HaShem multiply back to you a thousandfold what man has stolen.

Ben Ebner — for proofreading, text content advisement; and for being my patron saint of Suremomi'lltakealook. You are the perfect son — I adore you.

Molly Hurley (Teknigrammaton Graphics, Chicago, IL) — for hours of artwork; photos; advisement; last minute typesetting; taking care of all the business aspects of this project (I was clueless); for your undying love for and devotion to the Jewish people; and for persistently nagging me to call Paul when I almost dropped the ball. (And yeah, I still plan on being there when you're 89.)

Dana Lynn Joseph (Dallas, TX) — for masterful and soulful editing and suggestions; for your gentle, sensitive rewrites; for always being there to answer my questions; and for being my most beloved sister.

Rachel Williams — for extensive and excellent fact checking; for your tender, sweet heart; and for our time at the Bagel — I look forward to the years ahead!

Linda Wolf (Network Typesetting, Glenview, IL) — for brilliant editing; for gathering people to help make this book happen; for pulling more all-nighters than I can count; for your abiding friendship and love; and for that final moment.

Larry Zamba (Zamba Studios, Paddock Lake, WI) — for scanning and restoring photos of Paul's early childhood.

To all my family and friends who have been a source of encouragement and help — thank you. Especially to my father, Norman S. Joseph, who made life make sense and who I miss more than I can bear; Kris Daniel, Esq. (Law Office of Kris Daniel, Chicago, IL) for providing legal consultation and for preserving the enduring family soul; Khava Ebner for the beauty of who you are . . . always and forever, my baby; Mom and Norm for your love, support, and for always being there; and to everyone else in my life who has been diligent to pray for this book — I hope you know who you are. You're always in my heart.

A VERY SPECIAL ACKNOWLEDGMENT: To Professor Ken Waltzer, Director of Jewish Studies, Michigan State University — a huge thanks for your invaluable contribution to the second edition of *Number 176520*. The addition of your preface, your suggestions for textual inclusions and adjustments, the Nazi archive documents (on Paul) that you procured through the Red Cross International Tracing Service Archive in Bad Arolsen, and all of the accompanying historical information you have been so kind to provide have afforded this story the decisive legitimacy it both needs and deserves to stand as a trustworthy Holocaust biography in the world of academics, skeptics, students, critics, and victims. On a personal note, thank you for your kind words of encouragement and support. Our communications over the past several weeks have provided the impetus that has kept me going at times when I was tempted to give up. You are a generous and wise man, and I look forward with eager anticipation to the release of your book on the child survivors of Buchenwald. We still owe you a dinner, my friend.

Finally, I would like to acknowledge with utmost honor the millions of Assyrian and Armenian Christians who were murdered for their faith in what yet remains the most unrecognized genocide of the twentieth century. To my grandparents, Joseph and Khava Joseph, who were forced from their ancient homeland of Urmia, Iran, and to those of my beloved Assyrian family who remained and were martyred at the hands of evil men — may you find your rest and your reward in the shadow of the Almighty. *Libi milyahli.* ✿

Introduction

I first met Paul Argiewicz in December of 2005. The month had been an agonizing, emotionally charged marathon of days for me, and I was on the brink of coming unglued. All reserves of energy, self-confidence, worth, and purpose were depleted. I needed a cosmic connection. I needed to go shopping.

My husband, in his usual here-she-goes-again mode of mercy, dutifully escorted me to my own personal de-stress sector of the grocery store: the clearance dairy case. Little did I know, as I was having a meltdown over the familiar open refrigerator full of reduced foods, that I was about to meet a hero who would tell a story that would change my life forever — a story I would soon realize the whole world should hear.

As I obsessively dispatched dozens of ten-cent cartons of yogurt into my shopping cart, I perceived a presence at my side. Militantly fixated on my conquest, I lifted my eyes only when the presence spoke.

"You gonna take all of those?"

"Hmm?"

"You like bargains?" Standing behind his own cart that was packed with an admirable assortment of clearance dairy merchandise was a charming elderly man wearing a baseball cap and a delightful, mischievous grin. He had kind, sparkling eyes and spoke with an Eastern European accent.

"Bargains? Absolutely," I replied. "Where did you get the cottage cheese?"

"Over there," he said, without pointing a finger or turning his head in any particular direction. Judging from his playful grin and the vague nature of his "over there," I knew this enchanting soul was a hardcore competitor who wasn't about to divulge his secret. I had met my match. I found myself captivated by the man who had out-bargain-witted me. My mission of acquisition came to an abrupt halt as my attention shifted to a new, more intriguing focus.

"My sister lives in Sheboygan," he volunteered. "She feeds a lot of people, so I take food up to her. Here, take some cottage cheese."

iv

Succumbing to a nagging twinge of shame (I wasn't giving *my* food away), I tried to refuse his generous offer and politely but firmly shook my head. "No, thank you very much, but I can't."

"I insist; *please* take it." He pushed a carton of cottage cheese into my hand.

Having been raised in an ethnic home, the majority of my life was spent in the midst of strong, old-country, *very* persuasive people. I knew better than to risk offending my new acquaintance. I reluctantly conceded.

"Thank you very much, but only one carton. I don't want to take your food." I still couldn't help but wonder how *his* bargain radar had surpassed mine.

He was an unusually gregarious and pleasant person, especially for southeast Wisconsin. In more than a decade of living here, I could not recall even one time that I had experienced the pleasure of such a warm, even tender, encounter with a stranger. As we continued talking, I felt an inexplicable sense of adoration. Was it his amiable personality? Perhaps his accent, which reminded me of my beloved but long-deceased grandparents? Or was my thirsty soul simply responding to the kindness of a gentle and decent human being? Whatever it was, I subconsciously granted myself permission to bask in the genuineness of the moment. We talked for another ten minutes or so until he finally extended his arms to embrace both my husband and me as he wished us a healthy, safe, and prosperous new year. I wanted to wrap him up and take him home with us, but instead, we walked away.

"See how God loves you, honey? He sent you that nice Jewish man." My husband consoled me with a stroke on the back of my head. I yielded to the pressing emotion. Restrained tears began to fall as the stress of the past month melted away. I felt as though I had just been in the presence of an emissary from heaven. Maybe he was an angel, I thought.

"Why do you think he was Jewish? I think he was Russian or Polish." I lifted my fogged glasses to wipe the tears from my cheeks.

"No, honey, he's Jewish. Didn't you notice his hat?"

"Of course I noticed his hat. He was wearing a baseball cap."

"He was wearing a baseball cap ... that said *ISRAEL* on it."

v

"He was not! I couldn't have missed that!"

How the grocery items on the store shelves remained in their place at that moment is a small miracle; the sheer wind force created by the explosive U-turn of my yogurt-filled grocery cart should have knocked off the cashews and popcorn at the very least. The shift of the unfortunate people in my path resembled the parting of the Red Sea as I made a frantic beeline back to the dairy department.

I found him in the meats section.

"I'm so sorry. I didn't notice the *Israel* on your hat. I just wanted to say Happy Chanukah!"

"And Merry Christmas to you!" He turned, once again dispensing his charismatic, mesmeric smile without missing a beat. Then he picked up the conversation right where we had left it, but this time he had something besides bargains to share with me.

He rolled up his sleeve to show me something. There, on the flesh of his arm, was a tattoo.

It was a number.

The number 176520. ✡

Preface by Dr. Kenneth Waltzer

This story of a young teenaged Polish Jewish boy from Bielsko, Poland, offers a distinctive window into the Nazi Holocaust. Born in August, 1930, Paul Argiewicz inhabited and grew up in a world of peace, if marked by gathering storm clouds; but in 1939, when he had not yet reached the age of adolescence, the Nazis conquered Poland and Paul lived and learned to fend for himself in a world of flames. First ghettoized in Sosnowiec with his family, then separated from his parents and family, he was entered alone into the Nazi camps, where he existed and suffered from 1941 until 1945.

The Nazi Holocaust is generally understood as a planned extermination of Europe's Jews and other victims, including Gypsies. They were murdered by mobile killing squads beginning in 1941 or were deported to the Nazi death camps in Poland and annihilated using industrial methods beginning in 1942. Yet another part of the Holocaust, however, involved the simultaneous entry of hundreds of thousands of Jewish slave laborers into a new modern form of slavery in camps where they and others were subjected to terror, famine conditions, and brutal work. In these places, Jews were at the bottom of the Nazi racial hierarchy. Paul Argiewicz was among these slaves, spending four years or more in a series of labor and concentration camps, laboring for the Nazis and for Nazi firms.

Initially, Paul was selected at Auschwitz for labor before that camp evolved into an extermination center. Here he lied upward about his age, and he insisted falsely he was an electrician. He also spoke German. Then he was in several labor camps — on the autobahn, in Breslau, in Bunzlau (working for Siemens), and finally back in the Auschwitz constellation in Silesia at Blechhammer after it was transformed under control of the SS. In the end, Paul was on the death march from Blechhammer to Gross Rosen, a terrible place, and then was taken to Buchenwald, arriving in February 1945. He survived the final days in that camp when the Nazis sought to evacuate most prisoners and take them on the roads again. Although in the camp records he was listed as 20 years old at liberation on April 11, 1945, Paul Argiewicz had not yet reached his fifteenth birthday.

In Blechhammer, Paul had been tattooed with number 176520, where he worked as an electrician. The tattoo is a permanent legacy, as deeply inked in his arm as memory is etched in his brain. Later, in Buchenwald, he received another prisoner number, 126259, which he wore on his uniform and where he was in block 52, in the festering little camp. Because he was identified as older, he was not protected by the German Communist-led underground, which clustered mostly Jewish youths in a special barracks, number 66, located far from the SS gaze. So Paul survived on his own and by his own wits, resisting the Nazi efforts to draw him out in the final days. Liberation came from actions by the camp underground and by General Patton's U.S. Third Army, but Paul held on to life through hidden reserves of his own.

After the war, Paul searched in Poland and elsewhere for family, then came to America, settling later in Sheboygan, Wisconsin. There he developed into a special man who, save for the tattoo and the memory, lived well beyond the legacy of the camps. During the Holocaust, he had been taught in one camp after another to look out for his own survival, but everyone says he has lived since largely for others. Sharing his tale thanks to Deanne L. Joseph, turning his memory into narrative, is another gift to others — a portrait of experience in the camps and of human endurance and resilience and a window into a world we must never let recur.

Kenneth Waltzer
PROFESSOR AND DIRECTOR, JEWISH STUDIES
MICHIGAN STATE UNIVERSITY

Dedication

This book is dedicated in loving memory
to the millions of European Jewish men,
women, and children whose stories
will never be told.

We have not forgotten.
We will never forget.

CHAPTER 1

The Time Between the Great Wars

Bielsko bustled with activity. Known throughout Poland for its textile industry, the southern city on the Biala River was most famous for its quality worsted wools. Farmers raised and sheared their sheep outside the city limits in the countryside's green valleys. The wool was woven in the city's factories, then shipped to Germany to be dyed and processed. From there, it was distributed all over the world.

There was a healthy pulse to the city. In the shadows of an old castle that sat on a hill in the old city center, sharply dressed men and women crowded the busy streets as they walked briskly to work. Shop owners hurried to ready their stores for the new day's customers. Children raced each other to school. Life was good — or at least better than it had been. Poland was by no means thriving, but because of General Pilsudski's commitment to unify and strengthen his homeland, people were now able to find jobs and make a place for themselves in the world. After three hundred years of devastating wars, political unrest, and economic decay, the Poles of the 1930s could finally see a glimmer of light through the haze.

Noah Schwartzfochs lived on the outskirts of town. He was a strong, handsome, intelligent man with dark hair and captivating almond-shaped eyes. Born into an affluent Jewish family in Warsaw, he was the second oldest of four brothers. As a youngster, he had enjoyed a comfortable life with his parents and siblings. Over time, though, a twist of fate caused him to fall from favor with most of his family.

Two of his brothers, Simon and Gedalia, had become successful businessmen, married Swiss women, and moved to France. The youngest of the four brothers, Yitzhak, had escaped the political unrest in the country some years earlier and left for the United States, where he used his skills and education to climb the corporate ladder in banking.

Prior to World War I, Poland was part of Russia and all its young men were required to serve in the Russian army. Gedalia and Simon had already fulfilled their military duty and were no longer residing in Poland. Since

1

Yitzhak had left the country before his time of service, his call of duty fell to his only remaining brother. Noah was sent to Siberia for five long years to serve his "double duty." Forfeiting the privileged education his brothers had received, he fought in Russia's war against Manchuria. When he returned to his home country after the war, Noah was unable to secure a profession. Due to his lack of training and the catastrophic economic state of Poland at the time, Noah had to accept whatever jobs were available. Many were demeaning, time-consuming, paid very little, and certainly did not reflect his intelligence or his abilities. He eventually found work walking door-to-door, selling second-hand clothing by the pound. He peddled anything that might earn him a few pennies for bread or soup.

Against his family's wishes, Noah married a lovely younger woman named Elka Argiewicz. Although he was more than twenty years her senior, Noah and Elka created a pleasant life for themselves in the small rural town of Aleksandrowice, outside of Bielsko. It was situated in a green valley, surrounded by rolling hills, woods, and distant mountains. A river added to the mythical charm of the lush Polish countryside, and even though the town consisted of little more than sprawling fields, the small farming village seemed the ideal place to make their nest.

The rent was not as expensive there as it was in the city, and they were able to grow food in a modest garden. Tending sweet peas, purple garlic, and a variety of other fruits and vegetables kept the young wife busy as the newlyweds settled contentedly into their new life together. Elka bore Noah their first child in 1920, a daughter named Phella. Six years later Lucy came, and finally on August 6, 1930, Paul made his way into the world.

Noah and Elka had been married in a Jewish ceremony, but Poland, predominantly a strict Catholic country, did not recognize Jewish marriages. By law, the children of such unions inherited the mother's last name instead of the father's. While Paul got his mother's name, he got his father's penetrating dark eyes and crown of thick, wavy, dark hair. He flashed the impish grin of a delightful little rascal and proved himself a rambunctious, lively kid with a naughty streak that kept him glued to mischief.

From an early age, the Argiewicz children learned that life was not easy. Everyone had to pitch in to do his or her share of the work. Although

2

the family of five was very poor, they rarely went without food or clothing, and their home was a relatively happy one. Amid their contentment and the tranquil, fairytale beauty of their little town, however, an unthinkable evil lurked.

● ● ●

Poland was no stranger to anti-Jewish sentiments. For centuries, the Jews of Europe had suffered persecution at the hands of their gentile neighbors, particularly very "religious" neighbors. Though many Christians did not share in the bigotry, hatred, and irrational fury, they felt powerless to confront or change the hysteria developing on their continent. Attempts to defend their Jewish friends and neighbors were crushed by the insidious force of racism. Christians who dared to challenge the party line found themselves the minority, and at the receiving end of persecution.

For hundreds of years, Christians were falsely taught in religious institutions and communities that Jews were not to be trusted, that they were evil "Christ-killers," even that they used the blood of gentile children to make their unleavened bread for Passover. Sometimes the persecution was "mild" — disapproving glares, name-calling, and boycotting of Jewish businesses. At other times, though, the hatred became profound as Jews were subjected to beatings and ruthless violence. It could happen anywhere, at any time, for any reason. Anyone bearing a Jewish name or appearance was suspect — and a potential victim.

Poland was an especially fertile breeding ground for anti-Jewish sentiment. Many of its citizens were poor and uneducated, susceptible to faulty prejudices and inclined to accept them without question. Nevertheless, despite all the warning signs, no one — not even in their most unbridled imagination — could begin to conceptualize what was to come. For their part, the Jewish people continued in their daily affairs, hoping, if not believing, that the growing wave of hostility would pass and life would return to normal.

Many successful Jewish families lived in Bielsko. It was a wealthy and beautiful city where the Jewish community was known for its generosity in helping underprivileged people. They built a *kehilah,*[1] where children of poor

---

[1] *Kehilah* — (pro. keh-HEE-la) a Hebrew term denoting a religious community or congregation.

3

families, Jewish and non-Jewish alike, could go for hot meals. Paul and his sisters were only a few of the many economically disadvantaged children who benefited from the kindness and benevolence of that community. In addition to the *kehilah,* there was also the city's timeless and beloved synagogue; built in the late 1800s, it had been preserved in all of its ornate glory. Here the Jews of Bielsko and the surrounding towns met on the Sabbath, the holiest of days, to worship.

On Friday nights, the eve of the Sabbath, European Jews lit the *Shabbos*[2] candles. Together, they recited traditional Jewish prayers from the *Siddur.*[3] In reverence, they canted the familiar Hebrew words of praise,

> *"Baruch Atah HaShem*
> *Eloheynu Melech HaOlam*
> *Asher Kidshanu B'Mitzvosav*
> *V'Tzivanu L'Hadlik Ner Shel Shabbos."*[4]

Each year they celebrated the ancient Biblical holy days, thanking God for His provisions and His gift of life. They thanked Him also for sustaining them and bringing them to each new season of the Jewish calendar.

Noah took his family to the synagogue whenever he was able, although it was too far to walk and the cost of the train, though minimal, was more than he could afford. Instead, he spent time creating memories for his children at home. Though work demanded many long hours and much of his energy, Noah delighted in his family and invested as much of his spare time in them as his circumstances permitted. When he made a few extra cents and could afford the luxury, he packed the kids up and took them to a movie theater in town. Phella, Lucy, and Paul would sit for hours with their father, mesmerized by double and sometimes triple features. Occasionally, Noah was able to treat his children to ice cream cones — an unforgettable, thrilling extravagance that occurred only a few times during their childhood.

---

2 *Shabbos* — (pro. SHAH-bus) the Jewish Sabbath, beginning at sundown on Friday and continuing through sundown on Saturday.

3 *Siddur* — (pro. sih-DUR or SI-dur) a book of liturgical Hebrew prayers and blessings.

4 This traditional Hebrew blessing is recited every Sabbath evening as the woman of the home lights the Sabbath candles. Translation: "Blessed are you, Lord our God, King of the Universe, Who has sanctified us according to Your commandments and commanded us to kindle the Sabbath lights." It is generally followed by the *Kiddush* and *Motzi,* the sharing of wine and bread.

4

Most of their time together was spent at home. On their days off from work and school, Noah took his children for long walks through the woods, singing songs and telling them stories. He was always animated in his storytelling, making characters come alive. Paul and Lucy never quite knew whether what he was telling them was real or imaginary. It was of no consequence — they loved the stories just the same. They listened intently as their father taught them where to find the best wild mushrooms, explaining, "You will never see a fly on a poisonous mushroom." How to grow blueberries, potatoes, and other edibles in their garden; how to "witch" for water with willow branches; where to collect cheap materials to build such childhood wonders as a kite — Paul cherished the skills and experiences his father lovingly imparted and would carry them like a spiritual backpack throughout his life.

There were not a lot of extras for the growing family. Because most people did not have refrigerators, much less freezers, the children learned to preserve foods by canning. It was not a hobby — it was an essential task, a necessity for survival. Since food was often scarce, home-canned vegetables and fruits sometimes provided the day's only food, especially in the long winter months when business was slow and Noah was unable to sell his wares.

Their home had only two rooms: the kitchen and a modest bedroom that all five shared. Elka made a curtain from bed sheets to separate the girls' sleeping quarters from the grownups'. Paul slept wherever there was space — usually on the floor. A wood-burning stove in the kitchen provided the necessary heat for cooking and also doubled as the room's heat source. The family often sat in front of the fire, roasting garlic on forks; it was their "butter." In the bedroom, a coal-fueled 3' x 5' ceramic "heating oven" kept the family from freezing. On particularly frigid nights, a hot brick was wrapped in a towel and placed in the bed to keep the children warm.

On the rare occasion they could afford meat, it was usually chicken or duck. Because ducks were particularly fatty birds, their fat — like the garlic — was used in place of butter. Soup (made from a single potato and a few small vegetables boiled in water) or perhaps one or two baked potatoes cooked in the hot coals and ashes of the wood-burning stove became the basis of their diet. On a good day, they had bread. In a good week, they might have an egg.

Cow's milk was extremely expensive and was only affordable to the very privileged and wealthy. The less fortunate drank sheep's or goat's milk, from which they also made their cheese. Young mothers sometimes purchased human milk for their infants and toddlers, but when that was not available, underprivileged families fed the milk of horses to their little ones. When they were fortunate enough to have milk, Paul and his family always drank goat's milk. Occasionally, Paul enjoyed the luxury of drinking cow's milk at a friend's house. He much preferred it to what he was accustomed to drinking at home.

"Why can't we drink milk like *decent* people?" he asked his mother.

"What are you talking about? Of course we're decent people!" she replied indignantly.

"Then why do we have to drink milk from goats? It stinks!"

Fortunately for the poor of Poland, not only was goat's milk cheaper than cow's, it was also safer. An epidemic of tuberculosis was spreading rapidly, in part through the distribution of infected cow's milk. The TB bacterium did not appear to be present in the milk of goats. Every Thursday, the town folk purchased their groceries at the *Yarmark*.[5] They bought unregulated dairy products from local farmers, so the risk of milk or eggs being tainted was always a concern.

Traditionally, milk had been neither inspected nor pasteurized; it went directly from the udder to the consumer. Most buyers simply took the milk home and boiled it until a skin formed on the top. The process was thought to be sufficient to kill deadly bacteria, and people were satisfied that boiled milk was safe enough to drink. Unfortunately, it was not. As infectious disease began to spread among the population, Polish law eventually stepped in, requiring the products at the outdoor market to be tested. Government workers from the health department stood on the highways at the *Yarmark* taking samples of the farmers' milk, testing it for TB and other bacterial contaminants. If a sample tested positive, the entire vat was destroyed on the spot. Farmers who could not afford medication for their livestock lost their livelihood and became enraged at the bureaucratic intrusion.

---

[5] *Yarmark* — (pro. YAHR-mark) an outdoor farmers market where locals bought and sold goods.

6

In spite of all the hardships poor families experienced, children still enjoyed playing. And it was through playing that Paul and his sisters learned to speak German and Czech.[6] Bielsko was nestled in a valley on the border of Germany and Czechoslovakia, and the languages intermingled along with the people. Paul learned a particular dialect of German from some playmates from Bavaria, a region renowned for its expertise in brewing beer. A local brewery in Bielsko had hired a tradesman from the region, and Paul became fast friends with the brewer's children. They played together often, teaching each other their native languages, and it was not long before Paul developed a perfect Bavarian accent. As with so many seemingly trivial aspects of his youth, even his Bavarian German accent would play a critical role in Paul's later life. It was as though an unseen hand was weaving individual threads into a tapestry that would not be revealed for years to come.

Once a year, large mounds of coal were delivered to Polish homes. It was plentiful and the least expensive source of fuel for heat. One of Paul's childhood jobs was carrying the dirty black coal rocks to the basement for storage and keeping the ceramic heating oven in the bedroom supplied with the fuel. Because the coal arrived in large boulders, he would hammer it into smaller chunks, or briquettes, to fit them into the stove. The hard work was not without its surprises. Once, when breaking an especially sizeable piece of coal, Paul found a branch of a fir tree petrified inside. Proud of his discovery, he presented his prehistoric treasure to the school, where it was kept on display for several years.

Although there was ample water for cooking, cleaning, and bathing, Paul's home did not have indoor plumbing. Water was retrieved from a well. The children shared bath water in a washtub, taking turns bathing in the same water. Phella and Lucy, convinced that their little brother peed in the water, always insisted on bathing first. They had one bath a week.

Their "toilet paper" was newspaper that the kids tore into usable size pieces and nailed to the wall of the outhouse. Their outdoor "toilet" was outfitted with not one but two "seats" for those who did not mind having company while they attended to their private business.

Raw human sewage was collected by the tons every spring and fall. Because the Polish municipalities did not have sewage treatment plants,

---

6 At home, the family spoke Yiddish and Polish.

waste was removed from the ground in the cities and surrounding environs and taken outside the city limits, where it was dumped into farm fields. Within a few weeks, it was absorbed into the earth, forming the basis of a very effective fertilizer.

Very little was wasted in Poland in the 1930s.

It was a difficult life for Paul's mother. There was little money with which to shop and no modern conveniences to make her work easier. There was always gardening, cooking, laundry, and canning demanding Elka's time. She also frequented the town's bakery for the family's bread. Like the other women of the town, Elka would take her raw dough to the baker, who, for only a few cents, shaped and baked the bread. It was easier and more convenient to do this particular chore outside of the home. While their bread was baking at the store, the women scurried around town, running other errands. By the time they were done, so was their bread.

A *shochet*[7] butchered chickens and ducks for Elka when the family was able to afford meat. She cleaned and plucked the birds herself, always leaving the feathers on the wings — they made useful little dusters for the house. The skill of combining a little creativity with resourcefulness trans-formed many common everyday objects into handy, functional items and tools. A feathered chicken or duck wing became a duster (the remaining feathers were used to make pillows), animal fat mixed with lye became soap, a willow branch became an eggbeater, and a skein of wool was destined for a whole host of possibilities. Elka used wool yarn to hand-knit underwear and stockings for her husband and children. Because the wool was unprocessed, it was extremely rough and the itch it caused the wearer was nearly unbear-able. Paul detested his woolen underwear. One day at school, he scratched his body so furiously that the teacher was sure he had lice. She sent him to be examined by the school custodian. It was the zenith of childhood humiliation as the custodian explored and prodded every inch of Paul's naked body with a fine-toothed comb, searching for lice.

Noah spent his days traveling to the larger cities in Poland, Chechnya, and Czechoslovakia, scouring the areas for recyclable *shmatas,*[8] clothing,

---

[7] *Shochet* — (pro. SHOH-khet) a kosher butcher highly trained in the laws of kashrut (dietary laws of the Bible).

[8] *Shmatas* — (pro. sh-MAH-tuhz) a Yiddish term meaning "rags."

and other items to sell. He knocked on doors, day after day, hoping his wares would appeal to the wealthy residents of Bielsko and other affluent towns. He brought home an average of five dollars a week for the family of five to live on.

Noah worked too late for the entire family to eat together. The children would eat as soon as they arrived home from school. When food was ample, Elka and Phella prepared wonderful treats: noodles, bread, plum cake, apple cake. Sometimes Phella made her little brother a "Polish candy bar" by spreading butter on a French roll and shaving chocolate on the top. It was a delicacy, an unequalled experience in ecstasy for young Paul. The days always ended for the kids, however, on a less than pleasurable note. House rules mandated that they each consume a large spoonful of cod liver oil before retiring to their beds. Parents throughout Poland swore by this popular folk remedy.

In the warm seasons, one of the family's dietary consolations consisted of fish that Paul stole out of their neighbor's pond on his way home from school. When it rained enough, the neighbor's well-stocked ponds overflowed, causing the fish to surface. Paul was able to grab them easily with his hands. Once, when he had just pulled a nice carp from the pond and was making a mad dash home with his contraband, his neighbor caught him and began beating him. When the man's wife, a large woman who was chopping wood at the time of the incident, saw her husband assailing her youthful neighbor, she hurled her hatchet at her unsuspecting spouse. Luckily, she missed, and he released his beaten, bloodied captive.

The woman took Paul inside, cleaned him up, and gave him some warm food and a hug. She asked him if he might be willing to stop by after school two or three times a week to help her with some chores. He happily obliged, and for the next several seasons, Paul ran errands and did small jobs for the woman who was to become like a second mother. Before she would allow him to do anything else, she insisted that he complete his homework assignments. She went over his work meticulously, accepting nothing less than excellence. Only when she was satisfied that he had completed his homework to the best of his ability did she give him his job description for the day. She often scribbled a grocery list on a piece of paper, placed it with some coins inside a handkerchief, and gave it to him to take to the local grocer. Equipped with a little wagon for *shlepping*[9] the groceries, Paul hiked to and from the store, dutifully retrieving her goods.

The grocer who owned the store was a kind Jewish man who had a son named Bob. The boy was only a few years older than Paul, and the two became good friends. Occasionally their boyish disagreements led to skirmishes. One particular incident ended in a fistfight, and the normally mild-tempered shop owner chased Paul off the premises, pounding him on the head and back with a broom to get him out of the store. For the most part, though, Paul and Bob enjoyed each other's company and the two boys remained the best of friends.

Paul continued hauling the neighbor woman's groceries and doing odd jobs on her property. She, in turn, helped him with his homework, fed him sandwiches, and sent him home with enough fish for his family. It was a delightful arrangement. Paul even made his peace with her husband and carried buckets of pellets for him, helping him feed the once-forbidden fish. They strolled around the ponds, talking and sharing stories. As time passed, an unlikely but enduring bond of friendship developed among the three: the fish thief, the assailant, and the large hatchet-wielding woman.

● ● ●

While their father worked, Paul and his sisters attended school. There was neither public nor private transportation available for schoolchildren, so they walked together with friends year-round in every kind of weather. During the winter months, when the ground was covered with snow, they strapped skis onto their tattered boots and skied to school. Paul was thrilled to have a pair of skis but desperately needed a new pair of boots. Unfortunately, they were too expensive, so he made do with an old, exceedingly worn pair. In the warmer months, rain or shine, they walked . . . and walked . . . and walked. Only the wealthiest of children were able to afford bicycles and the Argiewicz kids were anything but.

---

[9] *Shlep* (Yiddish pro. SHLEHP) to carry or lug.

10

Goats, sheep, chickens, pigs, and other agricultural and domesticated animals roamed the streets as the town's children made their way down rough gravel roads and dirt paths to school. Dogs followed their young masters to the schoolhouse, barking and playing together outside the building until the children emerged at the end of the day. Paul had a scrappy dachshund that fought in the schoolyard with the other dogs while Paul fought with the other kids. He was harassed for being Jewish and frequently ended up in a tumble with his classmates.

The school day went from 8 a.m. to 2 p.m. every day except Sunday, year-round. At 10:00 each morning, the students were given milk and French water rolls with marmalade. It was a welcome and delicious fifteen-minute break. For lunch, they received a bowl of soup and a piece of bread. They were also vaccinated annually by a nurse and were entitled to very basic medical screening and care when it was available, compliments of the state. Because it was an agricultural country and disease was always a threat, the vaccinations kept tuberculosis, diphtheria, and typhoid from reaching epidemic levels among schoolchildren.

Inside the classroom, racial hostility was flaunted by teachers who made no effort to promote the education of the few Jewish children. The lack of attention was grossly reflected in their grades, as bright and promising kids like Paul lost interest in scholastics. Still, he attended faithfully for more than three years and made friends quickly, in spite of the occasional episode of harassment. Though he languished academically, Paul had some successes, as in second grade, when the class learned to weave floor mats from straw. Paul's became a permanent and functional addition to his home.

Every Polish school had a priest assigned to teach catechism, and in every classroom, a large crucifix hung on the wall next to a photograph of the country's president. A visiting priest once gave each of the Catholic children suckers; the two Jewish children in Paul's class received nothing. On Christmas, the catechism teacher gave his students large loaves of braided egg bread; once again, Paul was excluded. When the principal, a kind man who was not anti-Semitic, heard what had transpired, he called Paul into his office. "Is there anything I can do for you, Paul? Anything I can get you?" he asked.

"Yes. I would like to have some new ski boots," he answered without missing a beat. The principal smiled and sent him to the town's shoemaker, who made him a sturdy, beautiful pair of boots. Paul thought it must have been the best Christmas present a little Jewish boy in Poland ever received.

On their way home from school, Paul and his friends would amuse themselves by spying out people's clotheslines hung with laundry. They derived a great amount of pleasure from stumbling upon large people's underwear hanging out to dry. They laughed and poked fun at the sheer enormity of some of the more awe-inspiring undergarments.

City streets inspired this and other mischief. Around the age of seven, Paul began smoking. The little scamp randomly collected, lit, and smoked discarded cigarette butts from the dirty city streets. Because there was an endless surplus of cigarettes littering the streets, it seemed to Paul that every adult male in the town surely must have shared this tantalizing, macho addiction.

It wasn't long before Paul's mother discovered he had been smoking. She restrained a certain amount of her fury, leaving the job of her son's punishment to her husband. It was the classic "Just wait till your father gets home!" kind of day for Paul. After a brief dialogue with his nearly hysterical wife, Noah approached his young son. "So, I hear that you smoke?" Paul couldn't quite tell if it was a statement or a question, but the calm with which it was delivered took him pleasantly by surprise.

"Yes, I do." Paul never lied to his father — ever.

"Where do you get the money to buy cigarettes?"

"I don't need money," he answered innocently.

"What do you mean you don't need money? I smoke cigarettes and I have to pay for them." The understanding, sympathetic tone of Noah's questioning made Elka boil. Paul did not look at her.

"Well, they're free. I pick them up off the street." He volunteered the information with a sense of pride. This time his father's voice was not so calm; his demeanor changed and he sounded alarmed.

"What do you mean, you pick them up off the street? Don't you know about all the diseases you can catch? What if you get tuberculosis and die?" Paul didn't know how to answer. After a moment of uncomfortable silence,

12

his father continued. "If you want to smoke, I'll get you cigarettes. You want to smoke with me?"

"Yes!" Paul could hardly believe what he was hearing and could not have been more ecstatic. Enraged, Elka left the room, not realizing that her husband was formulating a plan to teach their son a lesson. He left the kitchen to "look for cigarettes." He returned with a cigar.

"I can't find a cigarette, so I'll teach you how to smoke a cigar. Okay?"

"Sure!" The eager seven-year-old watched his father's every move, suspended in heart-pounding anticipation as his dad sliced the cigar in half with a razor. Incising it with the skill of a surgeon, he handed half of the tobacco-laden treasure to his son. He lit Paul's half of the stump and offered instructions to his uninitiated student.

"Now, if you want to be a real man, inhale the smoke deeply and swallow the juice. It'll put hair on your chest."

In a matter of minutes, the seepage of sweat began to drench Paul's clothing. His father smiled and nodded as if to encourage the prolonging of his son's sadistic rite of passage. Paul persisted in inhaling the pungent smoke and swallowing the cigar juice until he felt too nauseous and dizzy to continue.

"Why are you sweating?" his father asked. Feeling ill and betrayed by his trusted ally, Paul excused himself to the bedroom. An excruciating pain in his stomach kept him awake through the night, and in the morning, his temperature registered 103 degrees. Severe diarrhea caused an agonizing, searing irritation on his rear end that immobilized him for the next ten days. His father's plan had worked. Having survived an ordeal he'd never forget, Paul was a new man. For the remainder of his life he would never again consider putting a cigarette, a cigar, or any tobacco product to his lips.

● ● ●

One of Noah's sisters, Lutvika (Aunt Lutka to the kids), was a successful veterinarian who had married Arthur Dubzhinski, a dentist who fixed the teeth of inmates and workers at the penitentiary. Like most prisons in Poland, the penitentiary was self-sufficient. The prisoners farmed fields of crops and tended orchards, providing food not only for themselves and prison workers, but also for the country's military units. The vast surplus of

13

potatoes, meat (usually pork), and assorted fruits and vegetables furnished soldiers with a steady and ample supply of rations.

Sometimes Paul accompanied his uncle to work. When approaching the prison, Arthur allowed his young nephew to pull the chain of a large steel bell, announcing their arrival to the guards. Because he was only a small child, Paul was permitted to enter the prison grounds and stay in his uncle's office for the day. Arthur wore a clean white shirt to work, and his patients, usually in shackles, would come to the office to have their teeth worked on. The instruments he used were old but sanitary, and he operated his antiquated drill by depressing a pedal with his foot. Everything at the prison was intriguing to Paul — the steel bell, the drill and other dental instruments, and especially the fields of food as far as his eyes could see. One warm summer day, a prisoner gave him a large bowl of ripe cherries freshly picked from the orchard. The dentist watched as his young nephew devoured the fruit, realizing with sadness how deprived he was, but unaware that the delight of this simple bowl of cherries would long remain in Paul's memory as one of the great thrills of his childhood.

Paul's Aunt Lutka worked for the Polish government inspecting livestock. The farmers who owned the livestock were unable to afford proper veterinary care for their animals, and the flesh of sick animals was often processed and sold in the markets. An epidemic caused by eating contaminated meat gripped the country. When the government finally cracked down on agricultural operations and demanded stricter regulations on meat, Lutka used her veterinary skills to acquire a job testing animals' blood and organs for disease. She had the difficult task of informing farmers that their livestock had to be destroyed rather than sold, causing many to lose both their farms and livelihood. The farmers reacted with hatred toward the bearer of bad news, and being a *Jewish* bearer of bad news compounded Lutka's already strained situation with the Polish farmers. European anti-Semitism continued to swell and had become a formidable presence in Poland.

Somehow, despite encroaching tensions and threats, Aunt Lutka and Uncle Arthur were able to keep their jobs and maintain their comfortable existence — at least for the time being. The devoted couple never failed to extend generosity to Noah, his wife, and their children. Every week, they

14

would send packages of food and other goods to help the struggling family. Nearly every summer, they would pay for train tickets for Phella, Lucy, and Paul to travel to visit them for a month or two. Those were the good times; unfortunately, they were not long-lived.

Noah contracted tuberculosis and was required to spend an entire year in a sanitarium. It was an extremely lonely, difficult, and stressful time, but Elka and Phella worked odd jobs to keep things afloat. The neighbors hired Elka to help them sell fish at the *Yarmark*. She helped transport live carp to the market, where the fish would be transferred to large tubs of water. When customers selected their fish, Elka would retrieve them from the tubs, decapitate them, and gut them under the buyer's scrutiny. Many of the wealthier people preferred to purchase their fish without heads, so there were plenty of carp heads for Elka to take home for soup making.

It was Elka's responsibility to keep people from touching the live fish in the tubs; they were fragile and often died from being handled. Once there was a customer who apparently did not appreciate taking orders from a woman. When Elka asked him to refrain from touching the fish, he pushed her. The unlucky soul regretted his infraction, however, when Elka promptly seized his cane and broke it over his head.

At home, Elka presided over her home with a firm but loving hand. Phella, Lucy, and Paul helped around the house, taking care of some of the chores. With the help of packages from Lutka and Arthur, the family managed to pull through the crisis of their father's illness and absence, and after a full year of confinement in the hospital, a recovered Noah returned home.

● ● ●

Phella gathered the family together one evening to announce her engagement to a painter named Pinchas Singer. Noah could not imagine how a "mere painter" would be able to take care of his daughter since everyone in Poland painted their own houses. "How can he possibly earn enough to support you? You will never have anything nice and you will always be hungry." He pleaded with her to reconsider. She assured him everything would be fine, that Pinchas was a gifted man and would be a good provider.

Noah wept as he reluctantly handed his firstborn to her groom. Though he adored all his children, she was the one who held the torch in his heart. How had time succeeded in robbing him of his little princess? Phella and her bridegroom stood under the *chuppah*,[10] as the seven blessings were sung in Hebrew by the cantor. The groom was elated. He stomped the wineglass under his foot as witnesses shouted an enthusiastic *"Mazel Tov!"*[11] Noah, grief-stricken by thoughts of Phella's future destined for poverty, misery, and hardship, abstained from the joy of the festivities. Paul had never seen his father so distraught.

As it turned out, much to Noah's surprise and delight, Pinchas Singer was not a "mere house painter." He was, in fact, a brilliant and famous artist. His paintings were in high demand and of such extreme value that one portrait bearing his signature commanded as much as Noah earned in an entire year. His prominence among the great portrait artists of Poland was a source of tremendous pride for the family, and his talent afforded the couple many luxuries that Phella would never have otherwise known. Beyond his artistic talent, Pinchas was a remarkable and generous man. After he and Phella moved to Sosnowiec, Poland, they frequently sent tickets for Paul to come to their home. The trip was a little less than 100 kilometers, a distance he traveled alone on milk trains. Pinchas purchased a beautiful home for his bride that, in the awestruck eyes of his young brother-in-law, surely must have seemed a palace. There, in his beloved sister's "mansion," Paul enjoyed unimaginable luxuries including an entire fish for himself.

Success, however, did not come without a price. Pinchas was often commissioned to paint disturbing subjects; some were political portraits that were especially egregious to the promising Jewish artist. He was once paid an irresistible $3,000 to paint an enormous portrait of a well-known contemporary figure. The man was seated high on a horse, flying a victory flag and wearing a Crusader's uniform. That man was Adolph Hitler. ✿

---

[10] *Chuppah* — (pro. KHOO-puh) a traditional canopy under which a bride and groom stand during the wedding ceremony.

[11] *Mazel Tov!* — (pro. MAH-zuhl tawv) Yiddish for "congratulations" or "good luck."

16

CHAPTER 2

The Occupation

Aspiring to create a *Judenrein*[12] nation, Germany's *fuehrer*[13] set out to unify the Aryan "blond" race. Hitler's disdain for people of color, racial ethnicity, and even specific anatomical characteristics added a heightened dimension of elitism to the already swollen ego of many Aryans. Blond hair, high cheekbones, and blue eyes became highly coveted traits. Masses of women flooded the drugstores, depleting the shelves of peroxide, as "peroxide blond" became all the rage. While the female population was scurrying to conform to the political definition of physical beauty, Hitler and his advisors were focusing their efforts on mounting a powerful military offensive against the rest of Europe.

In addition to his military aggression in the European theatre, Hitler was orchestrating a campaign against the Jewish people. The anti-Semitic violence that had been building broke out in a coordinated wave of destruction and death targeting Jews all over Germany and German-occupied lands on the night of November 9, 1938. It was one of the most devastating pogroms[14] in European history: *Kristallnacht.*[15] Hundreds of German and Austrian nationalists unleashed the fury of their hatred for the Jews, taking to the streets of their cities with clubs, stones, and axes. They smashed the windows of thousands of Jewish businesses. Many of the participants in the notorious pogrom sang hymns as they destroyed countless properties. Rioters burned synagogues and posted large signs reading "Don't buy from Jews!" They attacked and even murdered Jews in the streets.

The events of *Kristallnacht* launched Poland into a new fervor of aggression against the Jewish community. Inspired by the actions of their neighbors, the Poles were infused with a heightened boldness that sparked unprecedented hatred, resentment, and violence. University students congregated in major cities with inflamed residents to deal with "the enemy." Jewish men, women, and even children were indiscriminately attacked, beaten, and killed.

---

12 *Judenrein* — (German, pro. YOO-dehn-rine) a land without Jews; lit. "cleansed of Jews."
13 *Fuehrer* — (German, pro. FYOO-rer) leader.
14 Pogrom — An organized persecution or massacre of Jewish people.
15 *Kristallnacht* — (German, pro. KRIHS-tahl-nahkt) "night of broken glass."

The events of autumn 1939 would become the uncompromising force that would define the fate of millions of Jewish lives. It was then that Hitler's plan began to unfold in earnest. Germany invaded Poland. The impoverished Polish army was no match for the technologically superior German troops. The Poles came on horses; the Germans came in tanks. The Germans attacked on all frontiers and from the air. In less than a month on the timeline of human history, Germany achieved its unconditional triumph over the struggling country. Poland had been overrun . . . again. The victory was smugly coined the *"Blitzkrieg"*[16] by the conquerors, who wasted no time in establishing their authority on Polish soil. World War II had begun.

German occupation of Poland was not only immediate — it was merciless. Because Hitler vehemently opposed the idea of his subjugated people being educated, schools were quickly closed and declared "off limits" to all non-Germans. They were to remain in Nazi hands for the duration of the war — the next five years. German families moved in and took control of all educational institutions, taking full advantage of their facilities. Libraries, schools, universities, and all other education-related establishments were seized and placed under German control. Polish schoolchildren roamed the streets, immersing themselves in mischief and danger. Nervous parents attempted to entertain their children with activities that would keep them close to home and out of mischief's all-too-obliging path. Chaos won out, however, and reclaimed its position in Polish lives.

Non-Jewish adults continued to work, but only on a limited basis. Though they were still permitted to conduct business affairs, they were restricted by their foreign occupiers. Food, daily supplies, and imports were controlled and rationed. German police monitored and patrolled the streets, as all of Poland once again found itself on the receiving end of disaster.

Poles were furious and wanted to blame someone — anyone — for their calamity. The time bomb of historical repugnance for the Jew had been detonated. Reservoirs of malevolence catalyzed the Nazis' diabolical mission, and the brazen hatred for the Jewish people became a deadly common ground between Poland and Nazi Germany. Amid smoke-obscured shadows, an anti-Semitic demon emerged with unrestrained rage. Without

---

[16] *Blitzkrieg* — (German, pro. BLITZ-kreeg) "lightning war."

18

Poland's willful, even eager, participation in the process of "dealing with the Jewish vermin," Hitler would never have approached his goal of *Judenrein*. The occupied country became the medium in which the festering culture of hatred was cultivated. The culture saw its fruition in the construction of what would ultimately be deemed "the final solution" — and the death camps were birthed on Polish soil.

In the interim — before the concentration camps provided methodical extermination — Jewish businesses, community centers, and places of worship were restricted, closed, or destroyed. Jews were forbidden access to streets and businesses. As interrogations and beatings became commonplace, most Jews tried to keep a low profile by staying out of the public's watchful eye. Occasionally, however, Jewish people were "hired" to perform jobs for the Germans. Typically, these were the strong, young people of the community who were often never seen again.

All Jews were issued identification patches that were to be sewn onto their clothing. The original patch was made of white cloth with a blue Star of David[17] and the word *Jude*[18] printed in large letters. It was eventually replaced by the more familiar black patch with a yellow star. Initially, Jewish people venturing out without the identification patch were subject to arrest; later, they were simply shot.

The Jewish population found itself in disarray with nowhere to flee. Since they were forbidden to leave the country, only the wealthiest Jews were able to manage an illegal escape. Leaving all personal possessions behind, some fled to America or Australia. Others headed for their ancient homeland (what was then called "Palestine") via the "underground railroad" of Europe. Not unlike the enslaved Africans of America, they moved surreptitiously from one safe house to the next. Many traveled first to Czechoslovakia, and then through Romania and Turkey, before reaching their destination. Upon arrival, however, they were once again the unwelcome, unwanted people. Neither the British occupiers of the Holy Land nor the wealthy Arab landowners permitted the European Jewish refugees entrance into the Holy Land. Jews

---

[17] Star of David (Hebrew: Mogen David) — the most widely recognized symbol of Judaism, a six-pointed interlocking star.

[18] *Jude* — (German, pro. YOO-deh) Jew.

19

were forced to maneuver their way into the country through an underground network. It was a dangerous, often deadly journey, but those who managed to survive made their home in the existing Jewish settlements in the land. That good fortune was not typical for the vast majority of Europe's Jewish population. Like caged animals, they found themselves in a lethal environment — trapped, unprepared, and fatally vulnerable.

● ● ●

Like many other Polish cities, Bielsko suffered under Nazi occupation. Its vital, industrious pulse came to an abrupt halt as the imposing German aggressors transformed the beautiful town through a dark, seemingly paranormal metamorphosis. The city assumed a new persona; where yesterday Bielsko bustled with thriving businesses, today there was an eerie tension looming in the streets. The infrastructure of the newly budding glimmer of hope in Poland had been vanquished almost as quickly as it had appeared.

Paul was nine when Germany invaded his country. His father was now prohibited from peddling his wares and the already needy family became even more destitute. Poland's great leader, General Pilsudski, had died four years prior to the invasion. His successor was Edward Ryds-Smigly, whose incompetence was rivaled only by his extreme anti-Semitic sentiments. In much the same way that the country had succumbed to the Nazis, the Jewish population succumbed to unprecedented suffering under the new leader's racism.

Relentless nagging fear, want, and hunger pressed into Noah's home. Food, clothing, money — everything became scarce. Often the family went for days without a decent meal, and hunger pangs became an all-too-familiar foe. Schools were closed, work was nonexistent. For the next year and a half, life for Paul's family, and all the Jews of Poland, was reduced to desperate survival.

With resources extinguished, Noah contemplated his limited options. How was he to ensure the survival of his family? Arriving at what seemed to be the only prudent resolution, he gathered Elka, Lucy, and Paul around the kitchen table. How ironic that this spot — once a place of shared stories and carefree laughter — now saw their conversation dominated by the incomprehensible. They were to leave their home in Aleksandrowice and temporarily lodge with Pinchas and Phella in Sosnowiec. There, they might have a fight-

20

ing chance to keep disaster at bay until things returned to normal. It was too much of a risk for the four to travel together, however, so they would have to travel separately. Noah and Paul would pave the way, and, provided everything went well, Elka and Lucy would join them a few weeks later.

To keep maximum control in the country, the Germans had shut down all public train transportation. Noah and nine-year-old Paul had no choice but to set out on foot, making the nearly hundred-kilometer trek through the Polish countryside, towns, and cities with little more than the clothes on their backs and a few pieces of bread. Noah lied to his son: "I've already eaten; you take this bread." Always the devoted father, he gave his boy all he was able to offer — his own sustenance — and he hid his hunger from Paul. For more than two days, they walked, fighting thirst, exhaustion, and, most of all, constant hunger. They were determined to reach their destination alive.

When they arrived in Sosnowiec, they were greeted with grateful relief. "You're alive and safe! *Baruch HaShem!*"[19] Pinchas and Phella embraced them with a sense of desperation that Paul could not fully understand, but he was overjoyed to be back in their company. Drawing from the experience of his many idyllic visits to their home, Paul considered this a wondrous, familiar, and secure place. Familiarity, however, never dulled the youngster's sense of awe. Once again, he found himself in "the palace," overwhelmed by visible displays of wealth. The immaculate apartment was adorned with the finest furnishings, expensive rugs, and artwork. They sat at a table covered with embroidered linen cloth and ate from china plates. They even had a radio that received transmissions from Germany and Czechoslovakia.

Paul loved meandering through the apartment, examining the abundance of ornate objects. He was mesmerized by the Hebrew writing on the *ketubah*[20] that Pinchas' father, a rabbi, had lovingly scripted on his son's marriage contract before his untimely death. Creating a *ketubah* was an art mastered by only a few, and the perfection of the rabbi's skill was beautifully illustrated on the parchment. How proud he had been of his son, who had

---

[19] *Baruch HaShem* — (Hebrew, pro. ba-ROOKH hah-SHEM) a term of praise; literally "Bless the Name" (in reference to God).

[20] *Ketubah* — (Hebrew, pro. keh-TOO-bah) a legally binding marriage contract, the ketubah is a lengthy written document painstakingly hand-scribed in Hebrew on a large parchment. Adorned with beautiful and ornate artwork, it is frequently framed and displayed on a wall in the home.

been so blessed with the gift of art; and how deeply it had grieved him that the work of his son's gifted hands was remunerated by the very people causing so much Jewish suffering. His father was not the only one: It disturbed Pinchas profoundly that his lucrative portraits — still in high demand despite the Nazi-imposed ban on all things Jewish — were largely commissions to paint prominent Nazis and other political figures, particularly the *fuehrer*.

Elka and Lucy arrived safely two weeks after Noah and Paul. They all lived very quietly in the apartment, one day blurring into the next, as they passed their time reading, cooking, and painting. Paul and Lucy played hushed children's games together; they had to keep noise to a minimum. No yelling, running, or loud activity. It might draw unwanted attention. Like most Jewish families in Poland during this time, they rarely left the house. But they continued to hope, even believe, that tensions on the outside would lessen and that they might return to their normal lives. Instead, the serpent's deadly grip tightened even more, squeezing out what little breath remained in its prey.

One afternoon a loud commotion in the streets shattered the quiet. Noah took Paul by the hand and cautiously led him outside to investigate. Hundreds of Polish people crowded the area around the city's square, a sense of anticipation and excitement filling the air. Noah instructed his son to be very quiet.

"What's going on, Papa? Where are we going?" Paul asked.

"Paul, it's very important that you stay quiet. Can you do that? We'll just go a little farther until we see what's happening. Okay?"

Assembled in the center of the crowd was a group of nearly 150 teenage Jewish boys. They had been rounded up by the Germans and taken to the square. Everywhere, Poles hurled obscenities and shouted violent words at the frightened captives. Without warning, SS[21] officers drew their guns and systematically began shooting the young boys in the head. The shots continued until the last boy had fallen. Noah quickly ushered his son away from the scene, leaving behind a sea of blood-soaked stars of David on the earth. Horrified at what he had witnessed, Paul buried his face in his father's coat.

---

[21] SS — An elite unit within the Nazi party, the SS served as a special security force.

"Why did they do that, Papa?"

Paul did not understand his father's response: "Because they're Nazis — that's what they do."

Public executions soon became routine in Poland. Rarely did the Germans expend their energy beating Jews anymore — it was easier to shoot them. Still, no one could have anticipated the events of a quiet morning in 1940. An edict was issued for every Jew in Sosnowiec and surrounding towns to report to the railroad station in the city. No explanation was given, nor was time allotted for gathering personal possessions or making preparations. The mandate was clear and straightforward: "You will leave your homes and assemble at the station." A hushed murmur in the anxious crowd revealed their intense shock as SS officers rounded up individuals and families, herding them like cattle into lines to board trains.

"Where are we going? How long will we be gone?" No response. Questions dissipated into the air, and no one dared press the issue any further. The guards were ruthless. Anyone who deviated even slightly from their orders was shot or beaten to death with the butt of a rifle. The street was splattered with blood.

These were not the first murders this group of Jews had witnessed, so everyone knew better than to challenge the officers' actions. They understood that the same fate awaited any of them who might dare to exhibit anything less than absolute submission, whether perceived or actual. Defiance was out of the question.

On the train, the traumatized people spoke in measured whispers. Although the terrible reality of their situation was now unmistakable, they still hoped that the Polish army would regroup and ultimately defeat the Germans. Perhaps they were to be put to work for the war effort, they reasoned. After all, they were intelligent able-bodied Polish citizens with much to offer. If they could only buy some time by working diligently and not challenging the German authority, it was still possible that all would turn out okay. They comforted each other with these thoughts, clinging desperately to hope.

The train arrived in an impoverished area of Sosnowiec that had been sectioned off with barbed wire. Armed German police and SS officers guarded the gates and stood at regular intervals around the enclosed sector of the city. The Jews were unloaded and again herded into lines. A suffocating weight seemed to descend from the crowded, dreary buildings. This was the ghetto — the Jews' new home.

Families were permitted to remain intact, at least for the time being. They were assigned new living quarters in the dilapidated apartment buildings. Multiple families were put in one room, and conditions were vile. People had only the clothes on their backs and perhaps a few small items they were able to take with them on their unexpected journey. They were forced to sleep and attend to all of their private needs in the company of strangers. Because the Germans were obsessed with the notion of contracting disease from the "Jewish vermin" and thought the water supply might become contaminated, running water was accessible but barely adequate for drinking and bathing. There was only enough electricity for one light bulb per apartment — no heat, no refrigerator, no stove. Furniture was scarce and bathroom facilities grossly inadequate. There were few beds, pillows, or blankets to protect them against the biting cold of winter. On the rare occasion that food was provided, it was barely enough to sustain life.

The SS organized a committee of adult Jewish men in the ghetto who were to provide a workforce of young people from the "inside." The committee was given a description of the type of workers needed for each day, and they were required to round up the strongest Jewish youth to perform tasks for the Nazis. The young workers left in the early morning, labored all day, and returned late at night. Initially, they were compensated with minute rations of food; later they were compensated by being permitted to live through the day.

● ● ●

Simultaneously, the Germans were whittling away at the population of the ghetto, evacuating more than 5,000 people a day to make room for the influx of new Jews. The facts of the future that awaited them were unknown to the unsuspecting victims. The "final solution" was underway. In the early days of the ghetto, even the Jews' worst suspicions could not have contemplated the scale of the German plan. Men, women, and children were evaluated for usefulness and were moved out and transferred to concentration camps either to work or to be exterminated. Some camps were for labor, others for killing; most served both functions.

There were a number of concentration camps in Poland. They became populated with Jews, political enemies of the Nazi regime, and other "undesirables" who had been uprooted from their homes, forced into ghettoes, then transported to work camps designed to exploit their labor — until they eventually died of disease, starvation, exhaustion, torture, or were executed. For some, the labor camps were simply transit points to the extermination camps, the literal end of the line, where methodical mass murder was carried out.

Small children were killed immediately in the camps unless they were particularly strong or able to provide something of "value" to the Nazis. Some of the more attractive children were kept alive for officers' perverted pleasures, a fate that rivaled death. Others were kept alive for "scientific" research and experimentation. There were gruesome, painful, and exhausting experiments on terrified children, people with deformities and disabilities, and adults alike. Among many other "medical" horrors, people were literally frozen to death, locked in empty cells without food or water until they died of thirst, poisoned with chemicals and radiation, or killed by injection to the heart so that posthumous experiments could be performed.

●　●　●

Paul and his family lived in the ghetto for about a year. In spite of the dire circumstances, his boyish, adventurous nature remained. He removed the identification patch from his clothing and sneaked out of the ghetto through an opening in the barbed wire fence. It was an act of defiance that would have landed him at the end of an executioner's gun had he been caught, but somehow he was able to pull off this rite two to three times a week. Being the gregarious child that he was, he made friends with some gentile children on the "outside." They did not seem to mind that he was Jewish, and some of their parents even tried to help him in small ways. The father of one of his friends owned a bakery. The man's sympathetic conscience obliged him to turn a blind eye, allowing Paul to steal freshly baked bread from his store twice a week. The ritual continued for a year. Sometimes the determined young scavenger managed to find potato peels or other small provisions of

25

vegetables and was always faithful to rush his smuggled goods back to his hungry family behind the fence.

Eventually, Paul became so comfortable in his excursions that he inadvertently lowered his guard and came face to face with disaster. Returning to his family one day with a pair of stolen loaves of bread, he was approached by two SS officers.

"Where did you get that bread?" they demanded. Paul had never been so close to the enemy. He stood, accused and frozen.

"Come with us!" The order was stern and curt. They snatched the bread from his hands. The pounding of his heart intensified until he thought it would surely break through his chest. He could barely breathe. He felt a hard, squeezing pressure on his arm — the grip of a Nazi. He had the sensation of walking very quickly, although he was unable to feel his legs. Were his feet touching the ground? Were they even moving? He heard only the sound of the officers' boots clacking with each step on the hard street beneath their feet. His eyes burned as if on fire, and blurred images of his family flashed through his rattled brain. What would they think? Would he ever see them again? Were these men going to kill him? Paul fought to restrain the tears pooling in his eyes. He was only a child — his life was supposed to be ahead of him, not behind.

They arrived at their destination: an old schoolhouse that had been converted into a transitory evaluation and detainment center, the *Durkankslager.* He was taken downstairs to the basement, the "dungeon." It was filled with people standing in lines. Everywhere were the familiar Jewish identification patches. The Nazis pushed him into place with the others.

He looked around at the detainees, predominantly grown men. He did not see any other children in the crowded space. An SS officer sat upright on a stool at the front of the room, one leg raised and bent at the knee with his booted foot confidently perched on a table. Behind him was a desk filled with papers. As each of the accused men made his way to the front of the line, he was questioned by the man on the stool, evaluated, and sent into a group either to the right or to the left. Paul was not sure why the men were being divided, but as he drew closer to the evaluating officer, he was overcome with a sense of doom. His mind fired rapid, disconnected thoughts. "I'm only a

26

child . . . perhaps if I tell them I'm only eleven years old . . . maybe they will have pity and let me go back to my parents."

Without warning, a man behind him in the line kicked the back of his leg. He leaned into Paul's ear and spoke quietly but firmly.

"Don't tell them your real age. Tell them you're 18."

How did he know what I was thinking? Paul wondered.

He arrived at the head of the line. No longer did anyone stand between him and the "judge."

"Name?"

"Paul Argiewicz."

"Age?"

"Eighteen."

The words rolled off his lips in perfect Bavarian German. The officer looked up. His dusky eyes examined the youth before him. His brow furrowed, and he observed the boy for a moment. Paul felt as though he had been suspended in space and time. The moment seemed to last an eternity. Surely, he was exposed . . . guilty . . . he had lied . . . to an SS officer! The penalty for such an offense was execution.

"You speak German?" The officer seemed amused.

"Yes," he responded once more in the language he had learned from his playmates.

"You speak with a Bavarian accent. Why?"

"My mother is from Bavaria," he lied again. For another endless moment, the man's eyes pierced him. Paul was able to manage a convincing expression. Finally, the harshness of the Nazi's sharply featured face faded, yielding to a smile and a chuckle.

"Go over there," he said, nodding his head to his left.

Paul moved in the direction of the nod, but he did not understand the purpose of separating the men. Would he be sent to work or to the grave? None of the men seemed to know the fate that awaited them.

They remained in the detainment center for a few more days. Each day they were given small rations of bread and a cup of water. Paul allowed his mind to escape into a place of refuge and peace. He comforted himself with thoughts of his family, memories of good times they had shared, life in

Phella's beautiful home, and the hope that maybe he would soon be returning there.

In the corner of his eye, Paul perceived movement through a window in the damp stone wall. He turned his head to look through the dusty glass. Just beyond the tall barbed-wire fence, his father stood, his eyes scouring the room through the wire and glass. Noah's eyes found Paul's. His hand flew over his head waving to his son, his familiar penetrating eyes filled with longing. He held his hand still for a moment and then let it fall limp to his side. He stood motionless, his gaze fixed on his child.

Paul's heart raced within him. An overwhelming urge demanded that he jump to his feet and run to the window. He dared not. To do so would jeopardize not only his fate but also now his father's. Separated by brick and mortar, barbed wire and guns, and the merciless cruelty of the human heart, father and son looked upon each other for the last time. In that sacred moment, they knew that the bond they shared was beyond man's reach; it was a bond protected and preserved in eternity. Still, the eleven-year-old was overcome by the realization that he might never again feel the loving touch of his father's strong hands or hear the sound of his voice.

On the cold, hard floor, Paul covered his face and wept. His father was gone. ✡

CHAPTER 3

The Camps

Never in his life had it occurred to him to challenge the Almighty in His divine providence, but now Paul could not help but ask, "God, what did I do wrong that I should suffer like this?" What evil had he committed that led him to such an unforgiving fate? A barrage of questions and fears filled him. The most devastating thoughts were of his family. Would he ever see any of them again? What was to become of his father, the kind man who held all the answers to life's mysteries? And his mother, who so adored Paul that she called him "my *Kaddishil*"?[22]

He thought of Phella, the endless source of beauty, purity, and nurturing in his life. He thought, too, of her husband, Pinchas, such a generous, gifted, and brilliant man. If he concentrated hard enough, he could see them as clearly as if they stood in front of him. He closed his eyes, battling his weariness with their images. His sister Lucy emerged into focus — spunky and determined little Lucy standing close to her mother's side. He felt as though he could extend his hand and touch her silky brown hair. He conjured visions of Aunt Lutka and Uncle Arthur. Surely, he thought, they would fare well even in the frightening circumstances of the current world. They were successful, wealthy, and had valuable professions. He was sure they would be fine. He pictured the grocer and his son, Bob, and a hint of a smile came to him as he recounted their many boyish scuffles and adventures.

He drifted in and out of daydreams for a long time, suspended in the place of semi-consciousness where thoughts can be manipulated. Maybe, he comforted himself, I'm really asleep and soon I'll wake up in my own bed with my family in the next room. Perhaps fate was not so unjust . . . perhaps this was all merely an appalling nightmare. He concentrated all his efforts on making his thoughts a reality.

An abrupt nudge on his shoulder forced his eyes to open. "Here, eat this." A stranger held a small piece of bread in front of his face. It was his

---

22 *Kaddishil* — (Yiddish, pro. KAH-dih-shil) the person who says the blessing for an individual when he or she dies; usually the closest family member.

dinner. He was still in the *Durkankslager.* Good fortune had indeed evaded him; he was in the midst of the nightmare — and fully conscious.

After two days at the transitional holding center, Paul and a large group of other detainees were loaded onto an open truck. They were packed in tightly; there was no room to sit and barely room to move. As they pulled away from the building, Paul struggled to squirm through the crammed bodies, hoping to catch a glimpse of the outside. Perhaps he might see his father once more. Nothing. They stood, bodies pressed against each other, for a half-day's journey. The summer heat was unrelenting and there were no clouds to filter the sun's intensity. He thought he might suffocate in the crowd until finally they arrived at their destination. They were at a work camp.

Auschwitz / The Quarry

As they were unloaded and moved into more lines with more people for another evaluation, Paul noticed several rows of railroad tracks. He watched as boxcar trains pulled in, one after the other, to the entrance of the camp. Each of the cars was emptied of its contents by armed SS guards. Incomprehensible numbers of exhausted, frightened people bearing yellow stars of David poured out of the sliding doors of the cattle cars. Some of the cars revealed pale human corpses on the floors. Everywhere, myriads of Jews were being moved into lines, pushed, screamed at, and beaten.

Whispers filled the air, forcing their way uninvited into Paul's ears. What unpardonable sin were the Children of Israel guilty of this time that led the entirety of the ancient people to this present doom? Was the whole of European Jewry to be extinguished now — at the command of a lunatic — after all the ruin and tragedy they had survived for over three thousand years? They had endured hundreds of years of slavery in Egypt, endless wars and bloodshed in Canaan, deportation to Assyria and Babylon, the destruction of their holy temple and their holy city, Roman persecution, the Crusades, the Inquisition, Russian and European pogroms, inexorable persecution in the Diaspora,[23] and now *this*? Why were peace and safety so

---

[23] *Diaspora* — (pro. die-AHS-pohr-ah) the scattering of the Jewish people away from their ancestral homeland.

elusive? How was it possible that the world had become such a vile place, such a vast and hateful darkness? Paul tried in vain to force the murmurings from his mind. The weight was crushing.

In the crowd, nervous parents held the hands of children who were old enough to walk. They carried their toddlers and infants as Nazis herded them ever forward in immeasurable human lines. Teenagers, adults, and the elderly walked in silence. Young mothers and fathers spoke gentle words of reassurance to their young, but their eyes betrayed them, exposing an unspoken dread, an all-consuming fear.

A wooden sign read *Auschwitz.* The camp surrounding them was immense. It was rumored among the people that it had been constructed during WWI as a military base for the Austrian army. Paul had never witnessed anything of such magnitude. The furthest aisles of the infinite barracks stretched beyond his vision. He thought they must surely go on forever. The menacing barbed wire extended for miles without interruption, marshalling the lines of caged people. Some of the armed SS guards restrained snarling German shepherds on short leashes as others kept a vigilant watch over the enormous assemblage of prisoners from wooden towers. Everywhere, the ominous barbed wire loomed over them. The slightest idea of escaping such a place was futile.

Somewhere in the distance, beyond the visible barracks, the most insidious aspect of Hitler's "final solution" was taking shape: the infamous crematoria. The ovens where the corpses of countless Jews would be turned to ash were under construction. The sheer enormity of the camp, however, prevented anyone from seeing and therefore knowing about them . . . yet.

The reality of Paul's situation began to set in, and he was forced to consider the possibility that he would not be returning home — ever. The fleeting hope that had kept him from absolute despair was quickly dissipating. No longer just a "detainee," the eleven-year-old was now an official prisoner. He had acquired a new understanding of his current existence. If in the ghetto he had been deprived, now his life was devoid of the most basic human rights. In the camp, he was entitled to *nothing.*

Paul and the men he had traveled with from the detention facility were deposited into lines with thousands of incoming Jews and other prisoners. He maintained an uneasy quietness within the group, listening intently to the various languages as people began to converse cautiously. Several countries were represented in the crowd. Though most of the prisoners were Polish, there were also people of Dutch, French, Czechoslovakian, Romanian, and Hungarian descent. Beyond that, Paul was not sure. They whispered among themselves, the Jews predominantly in Yiddish, others in their native tongues. Most were able to manage broken German, attempting to communicate with those from other countries. They were hoping for information, some inquiring about missing loved ones, others simply wanting to know what was going to become of them.

The accused Jewish "criminals" stood alongside Jehovah's Witnesses, political dissidents, homosexuals, *Roma*,[24] and other "sordid undesirables." Because they were all despised in their native lands, they had been transported to Poland to work in the camps — or later to be exterminated. Notably absent from their company were the mentally disabled. They had been successfully disposed of at the outset of the war, as some of the finest, most advanced medical institutions of Europe acquiesced to the demands of the Nazi authority. "Euthanizing" patients with mental disorders was justified as an act of mercy. With the help of the hypodermic needle and later the gas chamber, much of the eastern part of Europe would rid itself of Down syndrome, mental retardation, schizophrenia, and a host of various mental, emotional, and genetic disorders. Hitler was well on his way to achieving his goal of creating and further unifying the perfect, "unblemished" Aryan race.

● ● ●

Prisoners were lined up, evaluated, and separated into groups. After evaluation, many prisoners, mainly the elderly and the infirm, were removed from the throng and never seen again. A Nazi's two-second visual examination was sufficient to determine the fate of a human being.

Paul was not questioned when he again lied about his age. "Eighteen," he told the commanding officer, and off he went with a large group of men

---

[24] *Roma* — gypsies.

32

to the barracks. Each man was given a small aluminum bowl that would be used for "meals." Inverted, it doubled as their "pillow." Every barrack was assigned a *kapo,*[25] a prisoner in charge of managing the others. The *kapo* did exactly as he was told. The only loyalty in this place was to survival.

The barrack walls were lined with long rows of bunked wooden slabs — their sleeping quarters. Paul and the hundreds of other male prisoners in the room found narrow spaces for themselves on the hard bunks. They had no mattresses, no pillows, and no blankets; just each other and their aluminum bowls. They tried to sleep, only to discover that the hard, cramped quarters did not provide enough space to stretch out. Each man struggled to maneuver his body in the clustered mass, attempting to create more room for himself while simultaneously trying to accommodate his neighbor. It was useless. The first night saw little sleep.

The *kapo* woke the men before daybreak the following morning. Their small bowls were filled halfway with watery oatmeal, or something that resembled oatmeal. When all prisoners were accounted for at roll call, they were sent to work. Paul fell into line with what appeared to be thousands of men. They walked for several miles before reaching their destination: the quarry. At the site, they were given wheelbarrows, shovels, and pickaxes. Under the watchful eye of the SS, they were forced to dig large boulders from the earth, break them into pieces, carry the heavy loads to their wheelbarrows, and transport them to lorries — large metal wagons on the train tracks. From there, Paul did not know, or care, where the rock was taken.

Some of the prisoners were highly educated men who had held esteemed professional positions prior to their arrest. They were doctors, lawyers, engineers, architects, scientists, and professors who were not accustomed to hard manual labor. Among them were old men who had miraculously survived the preliminary "selection." Many of them struggled just to make the walk to the quarry without collapsing. Their reserves of strength and health were already compromised and they were in no way capable of enduring this kind of physically demanding work. Many fell under the weight of the stones. Those who fell were shown no mercy; they were shot in the

---

[25] *Kapo* — (pro. KAH-poh)

head and died in the dust of the quarry. Within the first week, Paul witnessed the death of hundreds of men. Exhaustion, thirst, malnutrition, heart failure, beatings, and bullets claimed numerous lives.

Many of the guards in the quarry were Latvian, not German, but they shared a common lust for blood and the same disregard for human life. They entertained themselves by devising creative modes of torture and murder. In one of their "games," a guard removed his hat and threw it in the direction opposite a prisoner as the other guards looked on with laughter. "Run, Jew! Get my hat!" When the prisoner ran to retrieve the hat, the guard pulled his gun, shot the man, and then shouted a declaration to the rest of the prisoners. "He tried to escape. You see what will happen to you if you try to run?"

Refusal to obey a guard's orders only resulted in the same fate, although these prisoners were invariably made a public example before their murder. Beatings preceded the bullet; that was the rule in the quarry. Often, beatings were so gruesome that prisoners were dead or dying by the time the guard finally got around to shooting them. As a test of manhood, guards frequently egged each other on, daring one another to commit acts of brutality against the men. Prisoners were humiliated, mocked, beaten with bullwhips, clubbed, choked, had their skulls and other body parts crushed by rifle butts, and had their eyes gouged out with sticks or knives.

● ● ●

Nightfall at Auschwitz was a welcome reprieve. The lengthy walk from the quarry to the barracks was inconsequential compared with the grueling workday. The persistent wielding of heavy equipment and earth, day after day, coupled with nothing more than a small piece of bread and a bowl of tasteless diluted soup at night, left prisoners weak and starving. Some ate insects out of desperation. Anything that could even minimally relieve the void in the abdominal cavity was fair game. The threat of death became the only absolute; in an equation of endless variables, *it* was the constant. Survival exalted itself as the prisoners' new god.

Every muscle in Paul's body burned, his stomach ached from hunger, and bloody open sores and blisters covered his hands and feet. He felt sure that the exhaustion alone would be sufficient to kill him. He could not imagine surviving in this place. "What did I do to deserve this? Will You please get me out of here?" He submitted his desperate plea to the Master of the Universe. The reply was always the same: "I'm with you, Paul. I'm watching over you." The stillness of the voice rested in his soul.

Some of the older men offered him fatherly words of consolation and advice. "Just try to stay alive. If the possibility of a transfer presents itself, grab it! Get yourself out of here as soon as you can. For now, just do as you're told and don't give up. Try to make it to the end of each day. One day at a time, Paul — take one day at a time." A few men even shared their tiny portions of bread with him.

Paul's deliverance came two weeks after his arrival in Auschwitz. Men wearing business suits showed up at the camp, recruiting tradesmen for jobs at another location. What could a schoolboy his age possibly offer? He had no formal training in any trade, but was willing to say or do anything in order to get out of Auschwitz. Staying meant certain death. So when the request was made for electricians, Paul's hand flew into the air. "I'm an electrician!" he volunteered before even considering his words. "I'll go! I'm an electrician!"

Paul and several others were selected from the main group and ushered to the tracks. They were to be loaded onto a train just as soon as it was emptied of its most recent shipment of the camp's newest arrivals. Anxiously awaiting their departure, they moved through the masses of people who had just been deposited. Once on the train, Paul did not look back. Looking up at the ceiling of the car, he inhaled a long, deep breath. He held it for a few seconds until finally exhaling an almost indiscernible whisper. "Thank you."

The Train

The train carried its passengers across Poland's border into Germany. For several hours, Paul stood in the sweltering boxcar surrounded by the other prisoners. The heat mingled with the odor of sweating bodies, choking out any breathable air. Paul could barely inhale. It was crowded in the boxcar and their bodies were pressed tightly against each other. Many of the men had been imprisoned for some time now and were extremely thin. Their once muscular physiques were already severely atrophied from starvation and malnutrition. Paul thought their protruding bones gave them the appearance of skeletons wearing skin. Their darkly circled, sunken eyes were glazed over and staring at nothing in particular. He wondered if his form, like theirs, resembled a breathing corpse.

The wooden plank walls rattled and creaked as the train moved on the tracks. The hypnotic, repetitive clacking of the metal wheels swayed his mind to venture to a place outside of himself. As they traveled through the German countryside, he imagined how the scenery must look on the other side of the creaking wooden walls. His mind painted landscapes of sprawling fields and rolling hills, green trees and mountains. It reminded him of home. His eyes closed as a multitude of memories flooded his semi-consciousness. He embraced and guided them, placing himself in the kitchen at home in Alecksandrowice. His family members sat in their usual chairs at the table; his father at one end, his mother at the other, Paul and his sisters filling in the remaining spaces.

He entertained thoughts of food on their plates: of plum cakes, pudding, and Phella's Polish candy bars. An image of his grandmother's dear face flashed before him and he inadvertently laughed aloud, recalling a time when she brewed beer in their basement. The pressure from the fermentation became so intense inside the bottles that it caused the corks to explode off and fly around the room. The memory of the popping corks tickled his mind and he gave himself over to boyish laughter.

He drifted into other memories — to the "fix-it man" who periodically came through their streets with a pushcart full of tools and metal patches. The man went from door to door, offering to repair people's pots and pans, sharpen their knives, and sew or re-rib their torn and broken umbrellas. Women often brought their worn-out goods to the street, where he fixed them at his cart. Paul remembered, too, the vendor with a horse and buggy who folded pieces of paper into cones and filled them with warm peanuts and chestnuts. Though his family was never able to afford such a luxury, Paul loved the smell of the nuts in the air and the clip-clop of the horse's hoofs just the same.

36

He thought about his friends from school and the mischief they always seemed to unearth when they played together. How many hours and days had they spent collecting old alcohol bottles from ditches along the streets? When they had accumulated a sufficient number of them, they were able to make a few cents by selling them to the local junk dealer. With a twinge of shame, he remembered a classmate they had teased for being a bed-wetter. He knew better than to ridicule people, and the boy's incontinence did not seem at all amusing now. He wished for the opportunity to retract every childish thing he had done — anything that may have caused pain to the people in his life.

The faces of his family — of Noah, Elka, Phella, and Lucy — again floated before him. He tried to focus his concentration, to sustain the comforting apparition, but it was interrupted by the braking of the train. When it came to a stop, the heavy doors of the boxcar slid open. They had arrived.

The Autobahn

The Autobahn camp was small, not even remotely comparable to Auschwitz. It was guarded, not by ruthless SS officers, but by older German soldiers who were no longer fit for combat. Paul was encouraged; maybe they would be treated more humanely here. The group was showered, given clothing, fed bread and soup, and assigned to barracks. The *kapo* seemed a civilized enough man and Paul had his first good night's sleep since his arrest.

For the next several weeks, he worked in forced labor on the Autobahn,[26] laying electrical cable for the German superhighway system. It was a quiet camp and the prisoners were treated relatively well. That all ended when the SS arrived. They brought Polish political prisoners to the camp and, as always, screaming, beatings, and shootings accompanied them. After that, prisoners who fell down on the job were buried alive under the concrete of the highway. There was no mercy for the weak. Paul had to find a way out. He prayed again for deliverance. Within a week, he and the other Jewish workers were loaded onto a truck and transported out of the Autobahn camp southeast to the town of Breslau, Germany.

---

[26] The Autobahn — the German superhighway.

Breslau / Heereszeugamt

Heereszeugamt was a division of the German government that provided and repaired military supplies. Damaged war equipment was brought from the battlefields into Breslau by train and then sent to an enormous warehouse for repair or refurbishing. The complex housed row upon row of guns, ammunition, helmets, radios, and other battle and communication devices used in the war. Much of the equipment was German; it had been damaged in combat and required restoration. Some, however, was the property of rival armies and had been retrieved by German soldiers after the opposing forces lost it in battle. Weapons, ammunition, and other assorted military supplies were also looted from the bodies of dead soldiers in the fields. Occasionally, the company received entire shipments of brand-new equipment that was acquired when the soldiers of other armies tried to escape and abandoned their gear. Thousands of damaged German and foreign helmets were reconditioned, painted, and, along with everything else from the site, sent back to the front lines.

Since most of the countries involved in the war used similar — and in many cases identical — weapons and equipment, the workers used a kind of "mix and match" system of repair. If a German gun, for example, was in good condition but lacking one or two parts, they could easily remove those parts from an identical Russian gun, fix the damaged one with the spare parts, and have a fully complete, functional weapon. There was never a lack of military booty — especially from Russia — and the depository was in constant need of workers to handle the continuous incoming shipments. Prisoners bore the brunt of the workload at Heereszeugamt. It was one of the many sadistic ironies of the war; Jews and other prisoners of the Nazi industrial empire were forced to work on behalf of the very regime that sought their destruction. Through their compulsory labor, their enemy was being empowered. There was no time, no energy, and no desire, however, to consider the ultimate ramifications of such empowerment. Just making it through each day was as much as anyone could consider. The mind's singular devotion was to the body's survival. The body did as it was told. The soul was relegated to a state of sedation.

38

The concentration camp at Breslau was located a few miles from the factory. Like the Autobahn site, it was guarded by German police rather than SS. Fortunately, the police did not share the SS appetite for extreme violence or murder. In fact, the various sects within the German authority did not trust each other at all, and most of the police actually feared and hated SS. They, like the millions of Nazi prisoners, were also potential victims of SS cruelty and were often hanged or shot as dissidents.

Upon arriving at the camp, Paul was assigned to another barrack, another *kapo,* another life. Here, as at the Autobahn camp, the men were allowed to shower and were given a clean change of clothing. For breakfast, they received the standard watery oatmeal, and in the evenings after work, bread and soup. The soup at Breslau, however, had an ingredient that had not been added at the other camps he had stayed at. The prisoners referred to it as *dirgemeiseh*[27] — dehydrated vegetables that were traditionally used in livestock feed. Although it was neither a benevolent nor an intentional nutritional supplement, the *dirgemeiseh* proved to be a remarkable addition to the prisoners' diets. The vegetables rehydrated in the liquid of the soup and supplied the men with beneficial vitamins, minerals, and fiber. In addition, some of the local residents of the town sent butter and cheese to the camp. Paul felt strangely blessed.

He was assigned a variety of jobs for Heereszeugamt. For a while, he loaded trains with the reconditioned equipment that was to be shipped back to the front lines. He handled thousands of helmets, tires, skis, and even sleds for military horses. Some of his jobs required him to work outside, others indoors. But for that period it was all loading. Later, the eleven-year-old worked on grenade launchers.

One of Paul's jobs required him to unload scores of damaged motorized rubber boats from trains. According to the men he was working with, this job had a story attached to it: Hitler had his eye set on England, but instead of attacking from the sky, the Germans had attempted entrance into the country via the English Channel. Rather than risking the destruction of a battleship, they had used motorized rubber boats. A single ship could easily be taken

---

[27] *Dirgemeiseh* — (pro. DEER-geh-mee-suh)

39

out with one successfully aimed torpedo, but scores of armed soldiers in individual boats, they reasoned, would present a much more challenging target. British logic and strategy, however, had proven superior. As the German boats had approached their destination, thousands of gallons of gasoline were poured into the English Channel and set on fire. The Germans were unable to penetrate the smoke and flames. Some of the boats had been damaged beyond repair; those that had survived were shipped back to Heereszeugamt for refurbishing. Paul smiled as he helped to pull what remained of the soot-blackened boats from the train.

Large weapons were transported from one place to another on wagon-like artillery carriers called *lafettes.* These flat-bed trailers on wheels were capable of holding guns as large as cannons. They also had built-in metal drawers for the storage of artillery shells. Paul's job was to unload the drawers of incoming *lafettes* that had arrived from the Russian front. Drawer after drawer, he removed and boxed thousands of shells. He preferred this job to lifting and loading heavy artillery onto trains — it did not require the energy expenditure that the other assignments had. He had been losing weight rapidly, and although the prisoners were fed better at this camp than at the others, the quantity of food was still meager. They were barely given enough to stay alive, and the hard manual labor burned significantly more calories than the men took in. They lived in a state of unrelenting hunger.

Paul thought about food as he unloaded the artillery shells. He remembered how, after school, he had scoured streets and sidewalks outside of the city's stores for fish wrappers. Cod was the least expensive fish in Poland and vendors fried it, wrapped it in paper, and sold it on the streets. It was the city's most popular "fast-food" snack, and the grease-soaked wrappers littered the sidewalks. When Paul had collected a sufficient number of wrappers, the vendors gave him free fish. He could almost smell it.

The indulgence of the memory ended, however, as he began to open one of the *lafette* drawers. The contents felt different from the others he had been emptying. Something rolled and bumped the side of the drawer as he pulled on the handle. He exerted a little more force. The drawer opened suddenly, revealing a decapitated human head. It was the head of a German

40

soldier, still in its helmet, the decaying flesh being eaten by swarms of maggots. The rush of putrid air nearly caused Paul to faint. He looked up, panicked that someone else might have seen the contents of the drawer. He shut it instantly. As far as he could tell, no one had noticed anything. Any implication, from any person, that he might have had something to do with the death of this soldier would have meant his life. He did not speak a word to another soul about the incident. There was no one he could trust.

Camp Hubertland

After several months at Heereszeugamt, Paul was transferred out of Breslau to Camp Hubertland. Nearly a third of the next year of his life would be spent there. By age twelve, he had witnessed and been subjected to more horrors and abuse than most human beings experience in the totality of their years. He had been robbed of his childhood and his innocence. Nevertheless, as long as there was life, there was still hope. If only he could remember what to hope for . . . at least what to hope for beyond merely surviving each new day.

Thankfully, Camp Hubertland was also under the authority of German police, not the SS, so prisoners would at least stand a chance of being managed humanely. Paul's job included building and loading prefabricated wooden barracks onto trains. He worked side by side with French POW soldiers who had been captured in the war and were being held at the concentration camp. He enjoyed their company very much and found them to be especially friendly, helpful, and generous people. Furthermore, because they were soldiers, and not merely prisoners, the Germans supervised them with a great deal of care and respect. They were spoken to and treated with deference and were supplied with quality food, clothing, and other commodities. One of the POWs gave Paul an unopened pack of cigarettes for his smoking pleasure. Having learned his lesson about the woes of tobacco, however, he opted instead to negotiate a trade with another soldier and exchanged the highly coveted merchandise for a can of sardines. The French were frequently charitable with their food and Paul was grateful for their generosity.

Nearly everyone in the camp was able to converse in German. Many of the prisoners were not fluent but could easily get by with some broken form of the language. There was rarely a problem deciphering what people wanted to communicate. Week after week, they worked together assembling and loading war bunkers. One day bled into the next, providing neither hope nor purpose. Thoughts of his family persistently drifted through Paul's mind, always settling on the day that Noah waved goodbye to him in the *Durkankslager*. He could still picture his father's face; the sadness and worry in his eyes. It had been well over a year since he had been torn from everything and everyone he loved.

One evening in the barrack, the *kapo* approached Paul. He handed him a card from the mail. It read:

My son, Paul:
Everyone here is fine. Do not worry,
God will take care of you. We miss you.
Papa

It was the last Paul would hear from his father.

Bunzlau / Siemens

Any day in a work camp could bring a myriad of possibilities and changes. The next change for Paul came when a German company, Siemens, came to Camp Hubertland. It, too, was recruiting electricians for the war effort, and Paul volunteered for the assignment. Despite the fact that he had lost significant body mass, he was still young and strong and, therefore, in continued demand. He was shuttled by German police to Bunzlau, where he worked digging trenches in the woods and laying underground electrical cable. He also, on occasion, did cement work and performed various other assignments.

The camp itself was small, with approximately 150 adult prisoners, only a handful of teenagers, and fewer than five women (all of whom worked in the kitchen). The security guards were neither ambitious nor violent; they seemed to be interested in nothing more than running a clean, peaceful camp. Thankfully, there were no beatings here, and Paul was grateful to be in a place that did not impose a constant sense of dread or threat of death. Prisoners were treated fairly. They were given a daily ration of bread, soup, and water. They showered regularly and were granted a certain amount of freedom. In addition to his customary jobs, Paul was permitted to shine the guards' boots, earning himself extra portions of bread for the favor.

An elderly Jewish prisoner was appointed as a representative, an "elder," for the Jewish population. He was assigned a job in the camp's office, where he acted as a liaison between the prisoners and the supervisors. His concern and compassion for his people was unsurpassed, and he helped them in every way he could. The guards and administrators acted reasonably in their dealings with him and the entirety of the prison camp population benefited because of his generous and kind nature.

It was tempting to blame and hate all Germans for the evils committed against humanity during this period. However, there were some Germans, even a few within the Nazi regime, who were good and decent human beings. They were caught in a web of political insanity. One army colonel in particular demonstrated immense benevolence to the Jewish prisoners. When there were special functions or activities for camp personnel, he insisted that the prisoners receive additional portions of food — good food. When four SS men came in a Mercedes Benz to inspect the camp, he protected the prisoners by telling the officers that they were the best group of workers he had ever had. When prisoners were injured or seriously ill, he drove them into town and saw to it that they were seen by the best doctors. Whenever he was able, he brought the men extra bread and clean clothing — usually German army fatigues.

Life was better than it had been in a long time. The camp was clean, food was tolerable, prisoners were given soap for their daily showers, and the German authorities were not cruel. The guards were, in fact, so unassuming that the prisoners had to keep an eye on *them*. Periodically, they fell asleep while on duty and SS officers had a habit of showing up unannounced on routine checks. If the camp appeared too sedate, the SS did not hesitate to enforce their brutal authority. Guards who failed to exhibit "acceptable measures of force" could be removed from their positions. If they were caught sleeping, they could be shot or hanged on an officer's whim. Prisoners would

43

certainly not benefit from such a scenario, so they were faithful to alert the guards when the SS approached the camp. For appearance's sake, in those short periods, there were superficial demonstrations of pushing and yelling at prisoners, but it ended as soon as the "swine criminals"[28] drove away.

Although the company was an integral part of the Nazi war effort, Paul did not really mind working for Siemens. There was no way he could have known the extent of the company's collaboration in Hitler's "final solution" to the "Jewish problem."

For his part, Paul enjoyed being outside in the woods. It also afforded him a unique opportunity to shine in a way that was entirely unrelated to his post. There, in the forest, in the midst of trenches and cables, he discovered throngs of wild berries and mushrooms. They evoked memories of his childhood and all the times his father had taken him on long walks, educating him about the fruits of the earth. He took great delight in teaching the prisoners, most of whom had been city dwellers unfamiliar with country living, which mushrooms were safe to eat and which were poisonous and should be categorically avoided.

Paul ate as quickly as he could pick. Juice from blueberries stained his young, calloused hands, and he gorged himself until he was full. Indeed, his father's words seemed to be strangely prophetic and they rang in his mind: "God will take care of you, Paul."

He picked handfuls of rare mushrooms from the moist earth and used a needle to string the caps onto a strand of white thread. After drying them in the sun for a few days, he offered them to the guards. They accepted the youngster's offering with amused enthusiasm and took the prized fungus home to their wives. One of the guards returned the next day with a loaf of bread for Paul.

"My wife says these are wonderful; the best mushrooms she has ever had. They are extremely expensive at the market, so bring me some more. Be sure they are the same kind and I'll bring you more food tomorrow. Don't poison us, though, or I'll have to shoot you." Paul agreed to the deal and retrieved more mushrooms for the guard.

---

[28] "Swine criminals" was a term used by the German guards when referring to the SS.

44

Blechhammer / I.G. Farben

If Paul had to be at a concentration camp for the duration of the war or even for life, the Bunzlau camp would have been his choice, but the job ended and he was transported to another location. Almost a year had fused with eternity. He was sent by train to work as an electrician in a factory power plant at Blechhammer, a forced labor sub-camp of Auschwitz. His job there would require much greater technical knowledge and skill than he had thus far acquired, and he wondered how God would be able to help him this time.

The prisoners were counted, sifted, and assigned to barracks. Already, the horror was reminiscent of his first experience at Auschwitz. One group was ushered away; the second remained, awaiting further instructions. Paul was in the second group. For the first time in months he felt nauseous and had a familiar nagging sense of dread.

The prisoners were stripped of their clothes, their heads and bodies were shaved, and they were issued uniforms. Each person was given a cap, a pair of thin cotton pants, and a matching thin jacket. On each jacket was a colored stripe identifying the individual's crime. Jews: yellow; political prisoners: red; religious prisoners: purple. There were no socks, no underwear — just the cap, the pants, and the jacket.

Paul's mind rambled for a few moments. He remembered the itchy wool underwear and stockings that his mother had knit for her children. Thinking of home, though, no longer offered him solace, only pain.

At Blechhammer, prisoners were housed in wooden barracks, each one containing six rooms, each room holding 30–40 inmates. The rooms were overheated in summer and freezing cold in winter. The camp had virtually no sanitary facilities and included only one toilet and two baths in a separate barrack. The Nazis were unnerved by the prospect of lice infestation among prisoners (lice could lead to an outbreak of typhus), so they kept them clean with regular showers. *Kapos* and other workers hosed down the angled wooden bunks to minimize contagious infestation and the spread of potential epidemics. Prisoners were fed just enough to sustain life; no mercy was extended to the dead or dying and many died from exhaustion, overwork, disease, and starvation.

45

Paul was shuffled to a barrack where he spent the night. In the morning, he was taken to another area, where he stood in one of several lines with other prisoners. Inmate musicians were forced to play German patriotic band music as fellow prisoners were being processed. Little ones screamed as they were ripped from their mothers' arms. Some parents refused to surrender their young, fearing for their children's lives. Chaos would surely have ensued had the Nazis been less adept at crowd control. Instead, such situations were dealt with swiftly and efficiently, as noncompliant mothers and fathers found themselves at the barrel end of a German handgun. A single bullet to the brain, and the commotion ended. The cries of infants and toddlers faded into the accompanying music as the young children were carried to their deaths.

Paul stood quietly in the line, trying to tune out the sounds around him. He was not sure what he was waiting for, and no one spoke as the lines moved mechanically forward.

The Nazis had devised a unique system of identification to keep track of prisoners. Stationed at the head of each line was a man tattooing numbers on the arms of men, women, and the few remaining children. Paul stood in the line, awaiting his turn. When it arrived, he rolled his sleeve above his elbow, as instructed. The man used a needle to pierce the outline of a number into the soft flesh of his left forearm and poured ink into the bleeding wound. Paul became number 176520.

Everything in life had become so machine-like . . . so systematic . . . so numb. Human lives were reduced to numbers. Paul looked intently at the number for a long time before unrolling his sleeve to cover it. His youthful skin had been permanently marred and now bore a stain that would forever remind him of this defilement. He was no longer a human being, a child created in the image of God, a son of adoring parents, a brother, a nephew, a grandchild, a student, or a friend.

Paul Argiewicz was a number.

● ● ●

"Vernichtung Durch Arbeit" — annihilation through labor — was Blechhammer's motto. The cruel reality crossed all language barriers. By 1944, this was SS ground and they ruled it with an iron fist. The incarcerated

knew their place and most kept well within the imposed boundaries; those who did not were swiftly relegated to a place in the dust.

I.G. Farben, an enormous and thriving company of the Nazi empire, operated a power plant at Blechhammer. Several smaller companies leased space in the plant for the production of their manufactured goods. Here, over one hundred different products were made from coal, among them synthetic rubber (*"Buna"*) and gasoline. Gas was the most vital fuel for the German war effort, so bombing the manufacturing plants was a critically strategic offensive move for Allied forces. Whenever German factories commenced gasoline production, Allied war planes flew overhead, dropping bombs and causing extensive damage to the facilities. When they ceased production, they were exempt from bombings, but as soon as production started again, air raids sounded as the plants were bombed within the same day.

Having sustained repeated damage, I.G. Farben was desperate. In an attempt to conceal its gasoline production, the company implemented carefully calculated tactics to veil the plant. In one failed attempt, workers smoked out the entire complex of buildings in the hope that the Allies would not see it. They did, and the plant was bombed. On another occasion, they constructed a faux facility half a mile from the factory. It was built from cardboard and cheap secondhand materials; its purpose: a decoy for the actual site. The "buildings" were empty but gave the external appearance of productivity. Again, the Allies were not fooled, but they obliterated it anyway. The actual factory had two large smokestacks that betrayed the plant's location. As long as smoke was billowing from the chimneys, it was obvious to the Allies that gasoline production was underway. The company addressed the problem by disassembling and removing the stacks — to no avail. The bombings continued on a regular basis.

Paul was assigned to work under a middle-aged German man named Hans. With one leg shorter than the other, Hans was betrayed by a limp; a physical imperfection that prevented him from serving in the military. He accepted a position as a supervisor for I.G. Farben Industry and worked in the factory, overseeing hundreds of laborers. Among them were British POWs, political prisoners from countries that aligned themselves against Germany, and, of course, hundreds of Jews.

Hans treated his workers well and brought them disinfected used clothing to wear while they worked. Although he was an official member of the Nazi party, he neither shared nor participated in the party's commonly accepted views, beliefs, or tactics. He was a generous and compassionate man who had become a victim of the cruelties of the war and, in fact, developed a deep hatred for the Nazis. His wife, mother, and two sons had been killed in the Allied bombings of Dresden. Their home and city were destroyed when Winston Churchill exacted the revenge he promised to take against the Germans for leveling Coventry, England.

Hans took a special interest in Paul and over the next year assumed the role of a surrogate father. Every day he brought the youngster extra food. Paul had to eat it, however, in a remote closet of the factory so neither of them would be caught by the SS. Hans also brought him clean clothing when he came to work. Over time, he taught Paul skills that would ultimately save his life.

"You're not really an electrician, are you, Paul?" Hans asked.

"No." He grinned boyishly. He trusted Hans with his life.

"Okay. Well, let me teach you some things."

Hans taught Paul to wire electrical equipment. He kept him close to his side as he made his rounds on the factory floor, exposing his young apprentice to various skills and trades. Paul was a swift learner and in a very short time grew immensely in knowledge and ability. He learned to rewire and fix electrical implements that had been destroyed in the many bombings of the plant. His mentor was determined to instill in him the things he would need to know in order to survive the camps. Skilled laborers were in high demand, and those who were able to provide valuable services to the Nazis were often kept alive. Hans made sure that Paul became adept in a variety of trades, but in addition to teaching him proper skills, he also taught him to wire implements *backward.*

"If their equipment does not work, they will need electricians to fix it. As long as they need electricians, you will have work. Work is the ticket to life. Keep fixing their 'broken' equipment and they will not kill you. Remember what I've shown you."

Hans taught Paul everything he knew about being an electrician, and it was not long before the thirteen-year-old was operating and repairing intricate electrical equipment. He continued to protect, guide, and train Paul at the factory and Paul continued to work diligently. The two developed a bond that tempered an agonizing void in each of their lives.

Every day thousands of people came to the factory to work. In addition to the prisoners who were forced to labor long hours without compensation, there were hundreds of civilians from various countries who came to earn what they could. It was a heavily guarded facility and very few prisoners dared consider even the possibility of escape. *Vernichtung Durch Arbeit!* If not extermination through work, the bullet was always a faithful alternative. There was no vacillating in SS resolution in dealing with unruly or noncompliant prisoners. If one prisoner attempted to escape, hundreds were shot. If another did not comply absolutely with their demands, he (or she) along with several dozen others were made an example of in public executions. Prisoners were lined up against walls and shot. They were too thin, too exhausted, and too weak to exert the energy to rebel.

Even in their compliance, however, prisoners were never guaranteed being spared a bullet. Sometimes they were murdered for no other reason than a guard's bad mood on a particular day. Sometimes the guards, like those at the quarry, played games and murdered prisoners in a kind of sadistic contest. The SS needed no reason, no excuse, and no explanation to kill. Bodies were heaped into piles and burned in the ovens of the crematoria. Some were taken outside the camp and buried in mass graves in clearings in the woods. Those who were not murdered died of starvation, malnutrition, exhaustion, or disease. People died on the walk to the factory, they died at the factory, they died on the walk back to the barracks, and they died in the barracks. Death and hunger, hunger and death — these were the absolutes of every day in Blechhammer.

Prisoners walked through German villages, passing homes and shops along the way. Some of the women in these towns felt badly for the emaciated people walking through their streets, and they filled brown paper bags with food for them. They placed the bags behind garbage cans in the streets or in other areas where they knew the prisoners could easily access them.

49

Prisoners darted out from the moving cluster to retrieve the bags of food and other small gifts that the village women left and, just as quickly, retreated to their position before being caught.

There were, in fact, many who tried to help. Because Italy and Germany were allies at that time, Italian citizens came to Germany to work for I.G. Farben. Of course, they were compensated for their labor, but their alliance with the Nazis did not prevent them from demonstrating charity and kindness to the Jewish prisoners. Additionally, many of the incarcerated British POWs who were being held at the camp were caring and generous men. They, like the French prisoners at Hubertland, were managed respectfully by the Germans and were given preferential treatment. They received larger rations, better quality food, cigarettes, and medical care.

Many of the Brits shared what they had with the Jewish prisoners, who were denied such privileges. They smoked cigarettes as they worked at their jobs and dropped the half-smoked butts on the factory floor. Paul retrieved the butts, took them back to the camp at the end of the day, and exchanged them for bread or soup. He was astonished at how many prisoners were willing to give up their food for a smoke.

Prisoners worked as masons, welders, and electricians in the factory. Their hours were long, the conditions demanding. After serving as Hans' "gofer" (filling in wherever he was needed) and acquiring more advanced skills, Paul worked as a troubleshooter in the maintenance department. When he proved himself capable, he was assigned the task of installing high voltage lines and repairing wiring that had been destroyed in the Allied bombings.

When such attacks occurred at the factory, only the guards were allowed to take cover inside bunkers. Prisoners who were working outside were forced to remain outside, and many died from injuries sustained from projectiles and flying debris. Because Paul's job required him to carry expensive tools and electrical equipment, he was sometimes permitted to enter a bunker when bombings occurred. The tools were valuable to the Germans; his life was not.

During one of the bombings, a British POW ran for cover into one of the "privies" (outhouses) on the premises. While the makeshift toilet building did provide some protection from shrapnel — and ultimately saved his life —

it was not without its own particular brand of hazards. When the attack ended, the demoralized Brit emerged from the bomb-shaken haven covered head to toe in the black, dripping sludge of his countrymen's refuse.

Since Paul had lied about being an electrician and was still very new to more advanced tasks, the prospect of his new job was disconcerting. Installing high voltage lines was hardly a job for a novice, and certainly not something that a young boy without the necessary experience could handle. One mistake could mean his life and potentially the lives of many other people. The electrical lines were at the top of tall, splintered poles coated with cresol, a poisonous and corrosive compound used to extend the life of the pine poles. Paul had to climb the poles, maneuvering his way around the rough, toxic areas. It was a difficult job, but Hans saw to it that he was supplied with all he needed to perform it in as much comfort and safety as possible.

Most prisoners were issued shoes that were little more than pieces of cloth nailed to a wooden block. They provided no support, comfort, or warmth. It would have been nearly impossible for Paul to climb the poles in the issued wooden shoes, but Hans had convinced the SS to provide him with a pair of good, sturdy leather shoes with rubber soles so that he would be able to repair the lines efficiently. The shoes did indeed offer much-needed comfort, support, and flexibility for his job, but not even Hans could protect him from the dangers inherent in repairing high wires.

It was a hot summer in 1944. When Paul worked outdoors, he chose not to wear a shirt. A long, thick leather strap around his waist secured his body to the poles as he climbed. Once he reached the top, he shifted his weight, leaning back against the strap, and engaged a locking mechanism that prevented him from falling. He was then able to use both hands to do his work. Once, on a seemingly uneventful day as Paul sat high above the earth installing high voltage wires, he spotted an American reconnaissance plane passing overhead. He stopped what he was doing and focused his attention on the plane. His hope that it would continue straight ahead on its course was dashed when the pilot suddenly turned the plane around in the air and headed back toward the factory. Paul knew immediately they were going to be bombed.

Inside the eternity of a microsecond, he unlocked his climbers, leaned forward into the pole, released his weight from the belt, and slid down just as the plane fired upon the area. He ran from the site, the top of the pole crashing to the ground behind him. Within a few moments, the plane had vanished and he was left to cope with the aftermath of the attack. A severe burning in his chest drew his eyes downward. Dozens of sharp, deeply embedded cresol-soaked splinters impaled his upper torso. He closed his eyes, drew a deep breath, and returned to work. He did not dare speak a word of it to anyone — to do so would be a death sentence.

Despite the pain, he continued working through the day. In the evening, he walked with the other prisoners back to the barracks. The intensity of the stinging made it difficult to breathe. By the time he arrived at the camp, his body showed signs of cresol poisoning. His chest and abdomen were beginning to swell. He tried to remove the splinters, but they were buried too deeply in his skin.

Because Jewish prisoners were denied medical attention, showing his injury to the *kapo* was risky. The incident would have to be reported. That meant one of two things: he would be sent straight to the gas chambers, or the SS on-site at Blechhammer would simply take him outside and shoot him. Either way, he would be murdered, his body destined to disintegrate into ashes and smoke in a crematorium. Nazi Germany had no use for injured Jews. He had no choice but to lie on the bunk for the remainder of the night and endure the pain.

By morning, his chest was hot, red, and swollen. The threat of a potentially fatal infection skyrocketed and his odds of survival diminished with each passing hour. His immune system was severely compromised from malnutrition, and his reserves of strength depleted. The longer he waited, the more likely the toxic levels of cresol in his blood would reach a critical state . . . perhaps by the end of the day. He walked to the factory contemplating the gravity of his situation. The excruciating pain and his certainty that death was around the corner persuaded him to take a chance and show his wounds to Hans.

"Paul! Why did you wait so long to show me?" Hans hurried to the guard of the British POWs. "Go immediately and bring me a corpsman!" A

Prior to the World Wars, the boundaries of what we now refer to as the Eastern European countries were in constant flux. Consequently, reconstructing a political map of the region with absolute accuracy has been somewhat of a daunting challenge. Boundaries have moved, names and "possession" of cities have changed, and language barriers, as well as conflicting historical resources, have made our task difficult. However, we consider it not only a point of interest, but critical to Paul's story that the reader be provided with a glimpse into the great distances this young adolescent boy traveled, both in being transported from camp to camp, and also in the search for his family. We have therefore done our best with the resources available to recreate this map for that purpose.

Paul's Journey

1. Bielsko (Aleksandrowice), Poland
2. Sosnowiec, Poland
3. Auschwitz (Poland)
4. Autobahn Camp—Location Unknown
5. Breslau, Germany, now Wroclaw, Poland (Heereszeugamt)
6. Camp Hubertland (Germany)—Location Unknown
7. Bunzlau (Gross Rosen)
8. Trzebinia, Germany (Blechhammer)
9. Death March (Germany)
10. Weimar, Germany (Buchenwald)
11. Crimmitschau (Saxony, Germany)
12. Hof, Germany
13. Sosnowiec, Poland
14. Trans-Siberian Railroad (Russia)
15. Vladivostok, Russia
16. Return on Trans-Siberian Railroad (Russia)
17. Bielsko (Aleksandrowice), Poland
18. Traveled through Czechoslovakia
19. Hof, Germany
20. Traveled through Germany (for the UNRRA)
21. Czechoslovakia (to retrieve Lucy)
22. Bremerhaven, Germany (in quarantine)
23. United States

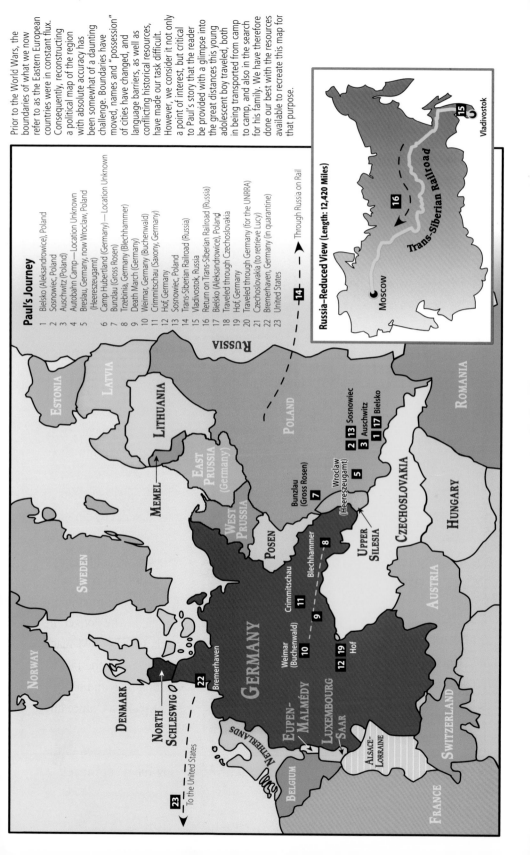

Russia–Reduced View (Length: 12,420 Miles)

Trans-Siberian Railroad

Moscow

Vladivostok

Holocaust Statistics

Country	Estimated Pre-War Jewish Population	Estimated Killed	Estimated Killed as Percentage	Estimated Number of Survivors
Poland	3,300,000	3,000,000	90.9%	300,000
USSR	3,020,000	1,100,000	36.42%	1,920,000
Hungary	800,000	569,000	71.13%	231,000
Germany	566,000	141,500	25%	424,500
France	350,000	77,320	22.09%	272,680
Romania	342,000	287,000	83.91%	55,000
Austria	185,000	50,000	27.03%	135,000
Lithuania	168,000	143,000	85.12%	25,000
Netherlands	140,000	100,000	71.43%	40,000
Bohemia/ Moravia	118,310	71,150	60.14%	47,160
Latvia	95,000	71,500	75.26%	23,500
Slovakia	88,950	71,000	79.82%	17,950
Yugoslavia	78,000	63,300	81.15%	14,700
Greece	77,380	67,000	86.59%	10,380
Belgium	65,700	28,900	43.99%	36,800
Italy	44,500	7,680	17.26%	36,820
Bulgaria	50,000	0	0%	50,000
Denmark	7,800	60	0.77%	7,740
Estonia	4,500	2,000	44.44%	2,500
Luxembourg	3,500	1,950	55.71%	1,550
Finland	2,000	7	0.35%	1,993
Norway	1,700	762	44.82%	938
Total	**9,508,340**	**5,853,129**	**61.56%**	**3,655,211**

Prior to and during WWII, Germany and Poland did not stand alone in the proliferation of racial intolerance. There were, in fact, many European countries that participated in the methodical mass murder of Jewish men, women, and children. Nazis were particularly diligent in their record-keeping; statistics and other documents continue to be released and updated to this day. The chart on this page illustrates some of the most current statistics available.

Paul's childhood home outside Bielsko, Poland

uncle in Switzerland. Pictured from left to right: Lucy, Elka, Paul, Noah, and Phella.

Above: **Family portrait, pictured from left to right: Paul, Phella, Noah, Elka, and Lucy**

Paul's kindergarten class: He and his oldest sister, Phella, appear circled in the back row.

Phella and Pinchas on their wedding day

Paul's beautiful mother, Elka Argiewicz

Elka poses for a picture.

Noah and Phella walk down a city street in Bielsko after his release from the hospital.

Bielsko Synagogue, which was completely destroyed by the Nazis in September 1939

Two views of Auschwitz

Larger photo: © Dreamstme Agency

Left: "Toilets" in the concentration camps

Below: A "standing cell" where prisoners were forced to stand still and silent while being bricked in alive

The smokestacks
of Auschwitz

Above: These bricked cubbyholes in the ground
are where the SS sat with machine guns,
waiting to shoot "unruly" prisoners.

Left: Concentration camp prisoner
uniforms *(see the following chart for
color-coded badge identifiers)*

Badge Identifiers for Concentration Camp Prisoners

Prisoners who were not sent to the gas chambers immediately upon arrival to the camps were forced to wear color-coded badges that identified their "crime" against Nazi Germany.

 Jewish "Race Violators"

 Jewish (Asocial Prisoner)

 Jewish (Political Detainee)

 Labor Re-education Prisoner (Asocial Prisoner)

 Polish (Political Detainee)

 Security Detainee (Asocial Prisoner)

 German (Political Detainee)

 Homosexuals (Asocial Prisoner)

 French (Political Detainee)

 Gypsies (Asocial Prisoner)

 Jewish (Common Criminal)

 Jehovah's Witnesses (Asocial Prisoner)

 Other (Common Criminal)

 Other (Asocial Prisoner)

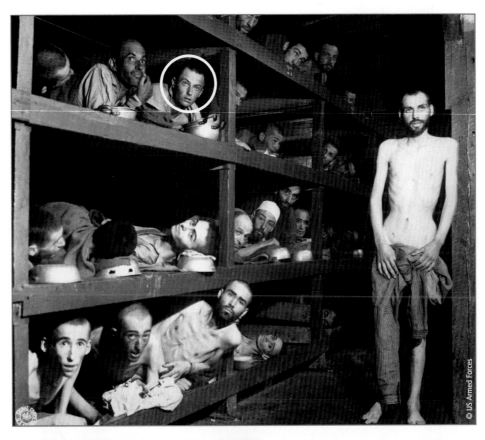

© US Armed Forces

Above: This well-known picture was taken of Buchenwald's near-death inmates about five days after the American troops liberated the camp. Paul Argiewicz is pictured (in the circle) on the top bunk. He was 14 years old. Nobel Peace Prize recipient Elie Wiesel appears on the slab beneath Paul, the seventh man from the left.

Left: One of the many gallows where the accused were hanged while other prisoners were forced to watch

Professor Ken Waltzer, Director of Jewish Studies, Michigan State University, obtained the following documents on Paul Argiewicz from the International Red Cross Tracing Service (ITS) in Bad Arolsen, Germany.

The existence of these and other documents has been invaluable in authenticating the testimonies of Holocaust victims. Additionally, these records provide permanent evidence of the Nazi regime's obsession with the political, religious, and personal—even genetic—aspects of individual prisoners. (Note that the numbers in the space after "Nase" are the measurements of Paul's nose.)

These scans of the original records have not been altered in any way. They are only nine of the 50 million documents housed in the ITS archive.

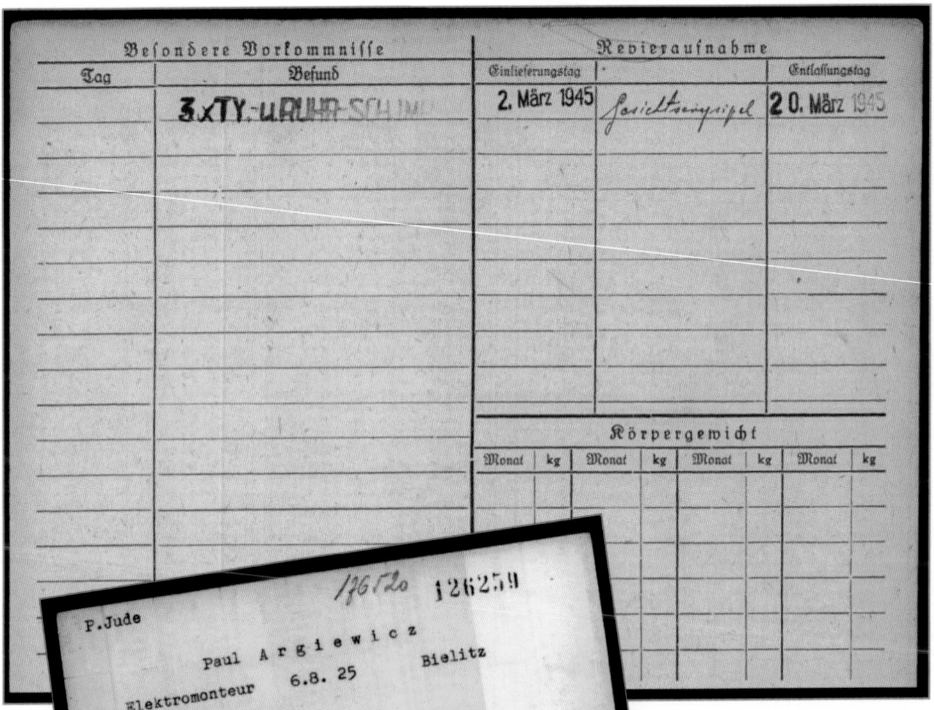

Besondere Vorkommnisse		Revieraufnahme		
Tag	Befund	Einlieferungstag		Entlassungstag
	3xTY.-u.RUHR-SCHUMP	2. März 1945	Gesichtsrotlauf	20. März 1945

Körpergewicht

Monat	kg	Monat	kg	Monat	kg	Monat	kg

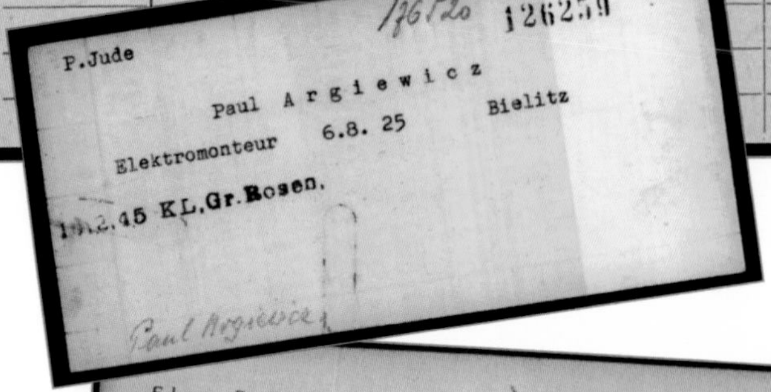

176520 126259

P.Jude

Paul Argiewicz

Elektromonteur 6.8. 25 Bielitz

1?.2.45 KL.Gr.Rosen.

Paul Argiewicz

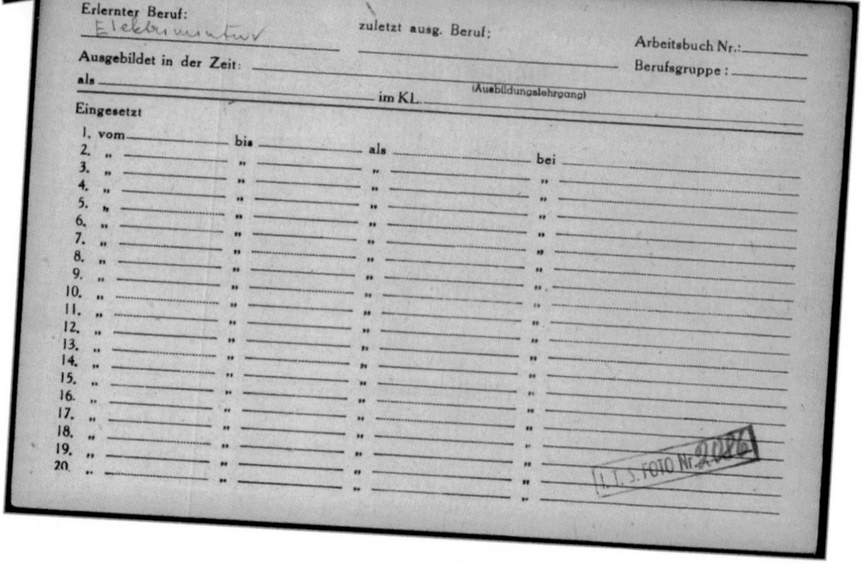

Erlernter Beruf: Elektromonteur zuletzt ausg. Beruf: Arbeitsbuch Nr.:

Ausgebildet in der Zeit: Berufsgruppe:

als im KL. (Ausbildungslehrgang)

Eingesetzt

1. vom bis als bei
2. " " " "
3. " " " "
4. " " " "
5. " " " "
6. " " " "
7. " " " "
8. " " " "
9. " " " "
10. " " " "
11. " " " "
12. " " " "
13. " " " "
14. " " " "
15. " " " "
16. " " " "
17. " " " "
18. " " " "
19. " " " "
20. " " " "

I. T. S. FOTO Nr. 2026

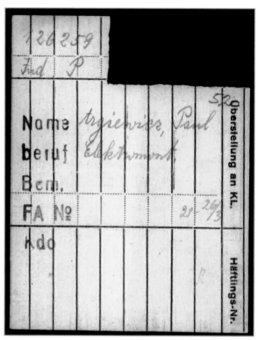

These documents on Paul were clearly created at Buchenwald, as evidenced by his assigned number at that camp: 126259. This number was not tattooed on his body, as was the original number—176520—at Auschwitz (Blechhammer). Rather, the latter number was stamped on his camp uniform.

Note Paul's recorded trade: Elektromonteur (electrician).

Pole 126259 Argiewicz Paul
Jude

geb. 6. 8. 25 Bielitz

Elektromonteur

1 0. 2. 45 GROSS-ROSEN

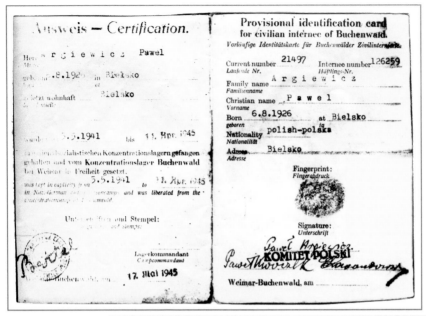

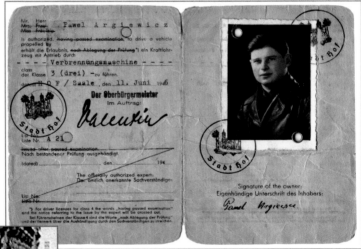

Top: Paul's identification card from Buchenwald (issued by the liberators): Note the recorded year of his birth, 1926 (rather than the actual year, 1930); also the designated "Christian name," Pawel; and nationality, "Polish" rather than Jewish.

Middle: Paul's German driver's license; age 16

Bottom: Paul in Hof an der Saale wearing Nazi boots and jacket—a gift from the "Beurgermeister"

Top: Paul in Germany with friend,
Chick Cooperman, the army quartermaster
of the American 76th Infantry Division;
Paul is pictured in the American G.I. uniform
he wore during his work for UNRRA.

Right: Paul working for UNRRA; age 17

Above: Paul (right) poses for a picture with an
American G.I. buddy in Hof.

Left: In Crimmitschau shortly after his liberation;
age 15

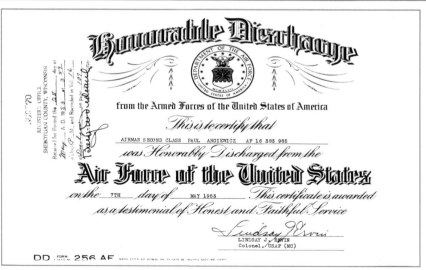

Top: Certificate of Naturalization (U.S. citizenship); age 25—considered by Paul to be his most cherished possession and accomplishment

Bottom: Honorable Discharge certificate from U.S. Air Force

Elie Wiesel and Paul met for the first time at a lecture Mr. Wiesel gave in 1999 at St. Norbert College, De Pere, Wisconsin. Although they shared the same bunk in Buchenwald, the men were too weak to carry on normal conversation and consequently never met until the night this picture was taken, more than 50 years later.

Left: Paul did not return to Poland until 2006. He is pictured here standing outside one of the buildings at Auschwitz.

Below: Paul and his wife, Cheryl, at a speaking engagement

Right: Paul is frequently invited to speak at schools, religious institutions, and various other organizations around the country. Although he was able to complete only three years of formal schooling in Poland, he has spent his entire free life studying history, global events, and a host of other subjects. Consequently, not only is Paul Argiewicz able to bring a face and personal experience to the gruesome realities of the Holocaust, but he is considered by many to be an historical scholar and expert on the subject. Once, when he had been invited to speak to a room full of theologians and students at a university, a priest in the audience stood and barked a hostile challenge, "What are your credentials?" Without the slightest wavering, Paul looked the man in the eye and retorted, "I have a PhD in common sense, you arrogant S.O.B.!" He received a hearty standing ovation from the class and the man later apologized. Paul is pictured here at one of his many speaking engagements.

Below: Paul and Cheryl Argiewicz pictured with author, Deanne L. Joseph, and Elie Wiesel at one of Wiesel's 2008 lectures

© Photo Courtesy of St. Xavier University

Paul and Deanne answer students' questions about the Holocaust and Paul's experience.

Below and following is a sampling of letters from students and others who have been touched by Paul's story.

Rabbi Tzali Wilschanski
Emissary of the Lubavicher Rebbe to Kenosha
Rabbi of Congregation Bnai Zedek Chabad

Bs"d

Thursday, 24 Tishrei 5769
Oct. 23, 2008
Greetings and Blessings!

In "Number 176520" you read the story of a young boy whose childhood goes from innocent, carefree, and loving , to witnessing and becoming part of one of the worst eras and stains on the history of the human race.

Pinchos is a man that could be anyone's Zaide. Always with a smile, a good word, a hug, even though he has led a life with more hardship and indescribable tortures than an average man would have in ten lifetimes. It is an incredible story, where one can clearly see the watchful eye & hand of G-d which was constantly with Pinchos. I had to finish reading the book in one sitting. All his experiences did not minimize his love and zest for life, and he remains the largest heart to fit in a human body.

Thank you Reb Pinchos for telling your story, thank you Cheryl, for encouraging him, and thank you, Deanne for writing this book and bringing the dream to fruition.

May the awareness and sensitivity that this story evokes make our world better, holier, happier and ready for Moshiach.

Very sincerely,   Rabbi Tzali Wilschanski

1320 N. Dr. Martin Luther King, Jr. Drive
Milwaukee, WI 53212-4002
Tel 414-277-4190
Fax 414-908-0327
bev.greenberg@twcable.com

Bev Greenberg
Vice President
Public Affairs

TIME WARNER
CABLE

September 26, 2005

Paul Argiewicz
6237 236th Avenue
Salem, WI 53168

Dear Mr. Argiewicz:

It was an incredible experience getting to know you and hearing your memories of your survival in the camps. You are a true hero and you have my deepest respect. Your willingness to share your stories with present and future generations is most courageous and we are all most grateful.

Time Warner Cable was proud to participate in the "Portraits of Courage" event. We have produced a video tape that we are pleased to forward to you as a keepsake of that historical event.

Thank-you for sharing your story. As you know, we are airing the event on Time Warner Cable's Digital Channel 1111. We are committed to ensure that the horrific events of the holocaust are forever remembered and never forgotten.

Warmly,

I wish you a Healthy Happy Holiday

Bev Greenberg

Your tragic story of workers digging their own graves and people being gassed will never be forgotten.

What stood out for me the most about your story was when you told us that not all the Germans were bad. It really made me feel better when you said that some of them had good hearts.

Sincerely, Kaleigh

Your story really inspired me to be extremely grateful for the life I am blessed to lead right now. I cannot imagine the terror that you had to endure. I will never forget you or your courage and strength to keep going even when you thought you could not. Although it is very depressing to learn about the Holocaust, I realize how important it is, and I will tell my children and grandchildren your story. I promise that your story of bravery will be passed on. This was an unforgettable experience for me. You are truly one in a million, Mr. Argiewicz.

Sincerely, Sarah

One thing that I'll never forget is how you met the Jehovah's Witness man who changed your life. I am a Jehovah's Witness and we still face persecution for our beliefs. Hearing you talk about us was heart-warming. I want to thank you from the bottom of my heart for sharing what you experienced in the concentration camps.

My grandpa was born in one of the camps and he has never spoken a word about what he went through. You have helped me understand what my own grandpa faced and I am so grateful for that. I'll remember you forever, Mr. Argiewicz.

Sincerely, Chloe

I can't believe all the poor, innocent people who lost their lives just because of what their religion was. The way they were treated was sub-human. It must have been awful to go out in search of food just to wind up never seeing your parents again. I know I never would have managed to go as far as you did, especially with no one there to support me or without any hope to go on.

I will never forget seeing your tattoo and listening to your stories. It was like I was there—watching you in your childhood—escaping death every day.

From: Kyle

This experience has been a real wake-up call for me. I really admire the way you had faith and never gave up. I could never imagine someone surviving something that terrible and when I hugged you I felt like I was hugging a hero. I'm never going to forget you, Paul Argiewicz.

Chrissy

Your speech and presentation was very touching. I am amazed at your bravery for standing up in front of us and retelling your horrifying story. I think I finally realize why survivors recall their stories: If you don't remember the past, you're doomed to repeat it. Without you I never would have realized that. I will never forget how your faith was the ultimate weapon against a force that chose violence. If you made as much of an impact on everyone else as you did on me your story will never be forgotten.

Sincerely, Jordan

I will never forget when I saw the number on your arm. I was in awe of how cruel someone could be to brand you like an animal.

Sincerely, Kaylene

At my school, my peers are always saying that they hate each other, but when those Nazis were so cruel to you, you were sorry for them! I will never forget that you were able to feel that.

It never said in our books that people were fed only once a day and that they couldn't get help or medicine when they were sick or injured. I looked at the pictures in one of those scrapbooks and I was shocked. I saw the hair, the glasses, and the gas tanks. Why did they do that? How <u>could</u> they do that?

Nick

One thing I will never forget about you is that even after the war with the Germans, you had the courage to join the army and fight for your new country. Mr. Argiewicz, you are very brave, and if we had more people like you I think that bad things would rarely happen. You are a great man with a big heart and I can't say these two words enough, but <u>THANK YOU!</u>

Sincerely, Michael

I read the book <u>Night</u> and learned much of what you said to us though that. Now, there's more of an emotional feeling inside me. It makes everything so much more real and scary.

Sincerely, Haley

I have had many hard times in my life. I have been to many schools and in each school I have been the outcast . . . the weirdo . . . the freak with no one to help me through. I thought I had it rough until I heard your story and realized how wrong I've been. I do well at hiding my emotion and my pain from others, but your story released a life's worth of unshed tears to spill forth. I hope that God grants you the greatest of blessings. I pray you live a long life so you can tell your story and inspire others as you have inspired me.

Love, Hannah

I still can't believe that you were separated from your parents at such a young age. Sometimes I have fights with my parents, but I would never want to be separated. I can't grasp the idea of losing them and I can't begin to comprehend the pain you must have gone through. Thank you so much for your time and your service to America. I truly believe that anyone who would hear your story, as I have, would salute you!

Sincerely, Emily

When you told me how your sister didn't recognize you I started crying. Also, you kept your tattoo so that you would never forget. Even though you went through all that pain, you never gave up. It inspires me to keep pushing forward.

Thank you for speaking to school students and for having your story written into a book. It's very important that these stories be told to children.

Sincerely, Jake

British corpsman's training was similar to that of a field nurse; he cleaned, disinfected, and bound wounds on battlefields. The guard retrieved a medical officer at once and brought him to examine Paul. The three men wasted no time in rushing him to the first-aid tent. It had been set up to treat British POWs who were injured while working in the factory. Hans convinced two German air-force men to stand guard at the entrance of the tent. They were to alert him at once if the SS should come anywhere near the area.

A buzz of whispers flew across the factory floor. "What's going on?" everyone wondered. Another medic joined them in the tent and, upon inspecting the cause of the commotion, approached the young patient.

He smiled at Paul and spoke softly. "This is going to hurt. Would you like a cigarette?"

"Yes, thank you." Paul tucked the cigarette in his pocket. He would take it back to the camp and trade it for food.

"You don't want to smoke it?" the soldier asked.

"Later," Paul replied.

The two men exchanged a smile and a knowing glance. "Well, how about a sandwich as soon as we're finished here?" the other corpsman asked him.

"Yes, thank you!"

Hans planted himself at Paul's side. He spoke gentle and reassuring words to him as one of the medics began to clean his bare chest with warm, soapy water. His eyes widened and he gasped, holding a shallow breath as the soap permeated the open wounds. The sting was nearly unbearable. The tissue surrounding the slivers had swollen, making it difficult to excise them without digging through his flesh. One by one, steel tweezers grasped and pulled the sharp, bloody wooden shards until finally the last one was removed. The man washed Paul's chest again, rubbed iodine into the wounds, and gave him a bottle of large black pills.

"These are antibiotics. Take two now and three a day for the next seven days. Do not let anyone see this, okay?"

"Okay."

He gave Paul a sandwich and a chocolate candy bar. It was a grand gesture of generosity. Paul was rarely privileged to enjoy such an extrava-

53

gance in his home, much less in a concentration camp. Indeed, he thought, God must be watching over him. Within a week, his wounds had healed and life — or some semblance of it — continued in Blechhammer.

● ● ●

Scores of Hitler Youth worked in the factory, diligently serving their government to ensure the *fuehrer's* dream: the millennial rule of the Third Reich. Beginning in 1926, teenage boys had been recruited, many hand-picked, for training under the National Socialist German Worker's Party (NAZI). Under Hitler's leadership, it was the only official youth organization of Germany, and at its height, its members numbered in the millions. Its purpose was best summed up in Hitler's own words in 1933:

> *"My program for educating youth is hard. Weakness must be hammered away. In my castles of the Teutonic Order, a youth will grow up before which the world will tremble. I want a brutal, domineering, fearless, cruel youth. Youth must be all that. It must bear pain. There must be nothing weak and gentle about it. The free, splendid beast of prey must once again flash from its eyes. . . . That is how I will eradicate thousands of years of human domestication. . . . That is how I will create the New Order."*

> — *The Final Solution* by Lawrence L. Graham [©2007]. p. 26.
> Cited in Walther Hofer, *Der Nationalsozialismus in Dokumenten* (National Socialism in documents) (Frankfurt am Main, 1957), 88

A blond Hitler Youth, dressed in uniform, approached Paul on the factory floor early one morning. Paul stopped his work and stood before the young Nazi-in-training. This can't be good, he thought. He was hoping it would be a peaceful encounter, but what could this brainwashed German elitist want with him? The last thing Paul needed was trouble.

In his hand, the boy held three silver watches, surely ill-gotten booty from Jews. He handed them to Paul without explanation.

And the boy had something else. "I found this," he said. "Would you like it?" The boy gave Paul a small, well-worn book.

It was a *siddur*. Many of the prayers were written in Hebrew, and although he had never really learned the language of his fathers, Paul accepted the treasure with deep gratitude . . . and relief.

54

"Thank you."

The boy nodded, turned, and walked away. Paul's curious eyes followed him for a few moments until he was out of sight. He tucked the *siddur* into his shirt and carried it back to the barracks that night. He would trade the watches for bread. They would help nourish his body; the *siddur* would feed his spirit.

"Will you teach me to read Hebrew?" he asked one of the rabbis.

"Of course!" The benevolent *tzadik*[29] was thrilled to have a student. It was a blessing to be entrusted with such a privilege. Heaven had given him an opportunity to share something that infused meaning and purpose into a young man's life — an opportunity he thought had been lost forever. What unspeakable joy this *mitzvah*[30] would be; the rabbi would bring life into a place that knew only death.

"I haven't had much schooling," Paul explained to his teacher. "I only went through the third grade before the Nazis came. I was arrested when I was eleven."

"Don't worry about a thing; you'll do fine. I'll teach you everything you need to know," the sage replied.

Each night Paul positioned himself next to the rabbi in the bunks, and letter by letter, he learned the ancient *Aleph-Bet.*[31]

● ● ●

It was September and the Jewish holy days were upon them. These were the most revered days of the year, days that had been given to the Jewish people "by the hand of Moses, from the mouth of God" more than three thousand years ago. Some of the nonreligious Jews had chosen not to observe these days when they had the freedom to do so, but their experience in the camps instilled in them a yearning to reconnect with their faith.

Rabbis quietly led Hebrew prayers and songs in the bunks at night and talked about the significance of the days. *Rosh HaShannah,*[32] they

---

[29] *Tzadik* — (Hebrew, pro. TZAH-deek) a religious, righteous man; one who keeps the commandments.

[30] *Mitzvah* — (Hebrew, pro. MITS-vuh) a "good deed" or obedience to a commandment.

[31] *Aleph-Bet* — (pro. ah-lehf-BEHT or ah-lehf-BEIS) the Hebrew alphabet.

[32] *Rosh HaShannah* — (pro. ROSH-hah-SHAH-nuh) traditionally accepted as the head of the Jewish new year; its Biblical origin was The Day of Blowing (trumpets).

explained, was the Day of Blowing (trumpets), the day that marked the beginning of the traditional Jewish New Year. *Shabbat Tshuvah* was a high Sabbath, a day of repentance, of turning away from sin and returning to God. *Yom Kippur*[33] was the Day of Atonement — the holiest of all days. The Ten Days of Awe were days of deep personal introspection that fell between *Rosh HaShannah* and *Yom Kippur*. It was believed that books in heaven were opened during these days and that the names of righteous souls were inscribed in the Book of Life for another year.

These were solemn days, days when the tribes, families, and individual souls of the Children of Israel were required to make peace with one another. Rectifying damaged relationships and restoring harmony was paramount during the Holy Days. At the end of the season was the Feast of *Succoth,*[34] or Tabernacles. It was an eight-day celebration in which the Jews were to live in temporary shelters (tabernacles, or booths) for a week, recalling the days when they were led by their prophet, Moses, out of slavery in Egypt. They recounted the forty years in which their ancestors lived in booths as they journeyed through the wilderness in search of the Promised Land.

● ● ●

The evening of *Yom Kippur* had arrived. The exhausted horde walked home from the factory under the dimming sky. Although the majority of Jewish men understood fasting to be a vital obligation on this Holy Day, starvation superseded conviction, and they did what was necessary to sustain life. In their present circumstance, that meant acquiring food whenever and wherever they were able to manage it. As they made their way through the towns, they slipped out of the group and grabbed food remnants from garbage cans. They snatched whatever they could find: lettuce leaves, cigarette butts, and scraps of pork fat.[35] Paul was able to dig up some potato peels

---

[33] *Yom Kippur* — (pro. YOHM kih-POOR).

[34] *Succoth* — (pro. soo-KOHT or SOO-kuhs).

[35] The pig is designated an "unclean" or non-kosher animal in the Torah (Bible) and is therefore forbidden as a source of food in Judaism. Other non-kosher foods include aquatic creatures lacking fins and scales (all shellfish) and any land animal that does not have a split hoof and chew the cud. Rabbinic law allows for the consumption of these foods only in the most desperate of circumstances, for instance, to save a life.

56

and little bits of onion. He ran back to the line, devouring his find. It was a bright, clear night and the first three stars appeared, marking the beginning of the Sabbath. What a perfectly beautiful sky, Paul thought.

When they arrived at the barracks, the rabbi opened the *siddur* and began to cant familiar haunting prayers. Some of the men listened silently in reverence, others sang along with him. It was *Kol Nidre*[36] — the night to make restitution for broken vows. The rabbi reminded them of days long ago when the ancient prayers held deep significance to those who canted them. During the Inquisition, the Jews of Spain were forced to choose between conversion to Christianity and being burned alive at the stake as heretics. Many refused to convert and were killed. Those who reluctantly capitulated to conversion were given the opportunity to recant the forced vows every subsequent *Yom Kippur.*

The rabbi encouraged the men to hold fast to their faith. He recounted the story of Masada, a mountain fortress in the Judean hills, where almost two thousand years ago hundreds of Jews chose to take their own lives rather than succumb to the demands of the Roman government. Men, women, and even children — entire families — voluntarily died at the edge of the sword, refusing to deny their faith. Those Jews who did spare their lives by avowing Rome's pagan culture undoubtedly brought comfort to their agonizing souls by canting the words of *Kol Nidre* or something akin to it; but in the mind of the faithful, losing one's soul was incomparably more tragic than losing one's life.

They listened intently to the words of the wise *tzadik,* but wondered how they were to reconcile this ancient belief with their present circumstance. Even the faithful couldn't help but question the rabbi: "Where is God now?"

It was somewhere around midnight when chaos erupted in the camp. The prisoners were roused from their bunks and forced outside. The moon was immense and shining gloriously, illuminating the earth beneath with an eerie glow. Its radiance was so brilliant that the scene nearly resembled

---

[36] *Kol Nidre* — (pro. kohl NIH-dray) a haunting piece of ancient Aramaic liturgy historically canted on the eve of Yom Kippur; lit. "All Vows."

daylight. The beauty of the hovering celestial surroundings, however, was subdued by an agitation in the air. Something was terribly wrong.

Looming before them in the moonlight was a makeshift gallows. Two nooses hung ominously from a crossbar at the top, a lone bench waiting below. The scaffold appeared crude in its construction and looked as though it would barely support the weight of a man. German marching music was played as two men, a prisoner and his *kapo,* were dragged to the stage. The man had been falsely accused of a "crime of sabotage," a charge frequently drummed up by the SS. When his *kapo* attempted to defend him, both were restrained, beaten, and pulled outside into the yard. Forced onto the bench, they stood convicted, side by side, hands tied behind their backs, as their executioners pulled the nooses over their heads. The ropes were tightened around their necks. The Nazis moved to the rhythmic beat of the music, entertained by their absolute power and imposing will.

A vigorous kick sent the bench tumbling and flying off the platform. The men fell, landing with a hard jerk at the end of the ropes. The length of the fall was not sufficient to break their necks and they struggled violently, their legs thrashing in the air for several seconds. Suddenly, the two hanging men fell with a cruel thud onto the stage below them. The ropes had broken under their weight. They lay, for what seemed to Paul like an eternity, coughing and gasping for breath as their executioners reset the gallows. The nooses were reattached to the bar and the two innocent men were hung again by their necks until they suffocated at the end of the ropes.

After that night, public hangings became a frequent occurrence at Blechhammer. The SS had created yet another sadistic tactic to instill fear in the minds of their captives. Some murders were committed to drive a point, others for SS entertainment, and still others for no apparent reason. Killings were often accompanied by threats to those who might consider anything other than complete submission to authority. Regardless of the motive, the Blechhammer Nazis derived a great deal of pleasure from the humiliation and terrorization of thousands of innocent Jews.

● ● ●

58

Despite Hans' efforts to keep Paul fed, healthy, and safe, his abdomen became severely distended and he lost body mass rapidly. For weeks, he lived with agonizing pain. His swollen, tender stomach began to contract until it regurgitated something into his mouth. He reached over his tongue and removed a six-inch strip of dense white tissue that he could not identify. Fearing that he might be dying, he showed it to a doctor who slept next to him in the bunks. The man informed Paul that in addition to starving, the problems he was experiencing were the result of tapeworm infestation. What he held in his hand was a segment of a tapeworm.

The kindly doctor explained to him that if he did not expel the entire parasite, preferably intact, he would likely die. To accomplish the feat, he would have to induce abdominal contractions; it was the only way to rid his body of the worm. Otherwise, it would continue consuming the little nutrition he was getting until he died of starvation. From the doctor's vantage point, that looked to be only a matter of days.

He taught Paul how to tense his abdominal muscles in such a way as to force the worm out of his body through his mouth. Immediately, Paul began to gag and retch, his stomach succumbing to violent involuntary contractions. It was hard to catch his breath. When he felt the head of the worm enter his mouth, he carefully seized it and began to pull slowly and gingerly, all the while maintaining strong tension in his muscles. He released the worm from his fingers to avoid tearing it and allowed the contractions to complete the repugnant task.

He tried to control the gagging reflex as he continued expelling the worm from his belly and out his mouth. Finally, he successfully extracted the long white worm. It was still alive. It measured more than three feet long and was as wide around as his finger. He looked for a few moments at the parasite and thought to himself that if he had not already been sick to his stomach, surely the sight of this thing was sufficient to have made him so. The doctor examined the specimen.

He smiled at his patient, gently rubbing the back of Paul's shoulder while offering words of consolation. *"Baruch HaShem!* You did well — you got the whole thing! You will feel better now, you'll see." ✿

CHAPTER 4

The Death March from Blechhammer to Gross Rosen

By the end of 1944, Russian troops had penetrated the German border and were approaching the huge Nazi complex at Auschwitz. The war had proven devastating to Germany — the severe loss of troops, property, and supplies had left its seemingly invincible military in shambles. Adolph Hitler's indomitable infrastructure was beginning to crumble. The Russians took no pity on the SS; immediately upon capture and positive identification, they were shot — no questions asked. In contrast, German soldiers were detained in prisoner-of-war camps. Because military personnel were permitted to live, SS guards confiscated army uniforms and attempted to pass themselves off as soldiers. In most cases, though, their ploys were unsuccessful. Their rank was easily verified by a mandatory identification tattoo in the armpit. It revealed the officer's rank and blood type.

Remaining members of the Nazi regime scrambled to escape the country. Before leaving, however, they embarked on a swift mission to evacuate any camps whose prisoners might fall into the hands of the enemy and to raze to the ground anything that would expose the extensiveness of their murderous criminal activity. Orders from lingering authority mandated that all incriminating evidence be destroyed without delay. Prisoners were removed from barracks and factories and told they were to be transferred to another camp. In actuality, while many were rounded up, evacuated, and marched to rail heads where they could, in turn, be transported to camps in Germany, others were taken to areas for extermination. The SS led many into surrounding woods to clearings where they were shot and bulldozed into mass graves. Thousands died.

● ● ●

It was a frigid January morning in 1945, just before dawn, when orders were given to evacuate Blechhammer. The prisoners were roused and instructed to collect their soup bowls. They were taken outside. There, each man was given a piece of bread and told to wait for further instructions.

61

Above them in the near distance, graceful fractal patterns of bare treetops were silhouetted against the soft pastels of the winter sunrise. The contrast between the two worlds surpassed irony — it was absurd. How was it possible to display, within only a few feet, the supremacy of Nature's inexhaustible beauty and the zenith of human depravity?

Armed guards seemed particularly agitated as they stormed through the yard, screaming and beating dying prisoners. Prisoners were beyond wondering what was happening and many no longer cared — they just wanted peace. If that meant death, so be it. Some, mostly the young, still clung to life. Their bony, shivering fingers held the bread tightly to their chests. They were determined not to give in to the temptation of indifference. To do so would have meant certain death, and they still had, in the core of their souls, the will to defy it. They stood silently, clothed in the standard prison camp uniform — the same thin, worn striped cotton pants and shirt that had been issued when they arrived at Blechhammer. On their feet were the same shoes, the blocks of wood now badly worn, with nothing more than a narrow strip of tattered fabric to cover the top of the foot. Already they were freezing in the biting air. The bitter winter wind howled around them.

In previous weeks, as temperatures dropped, Paul and some of the other factory workers learned to use discarded 100-pound cement bags as insulation under their clothing. Prisoners had lived in a state of sustained starvation for so long that they no longer had the necessary body fat to shield or insulate their withered forms. The heavy paper bags were several layers thick and provided some protection against the bitter days and nights. They removed the dusty inside layers of the bags, cut holes for their heads and arms, and slipped them onto their bodies. Tying a rope around the waist trapped at least a minimal amount of essential body heat, protecting their kidneys and other vital organs. (A doctor who was also a prisoner in the camp had instructed Paul to keep his kidneys warm.) Their shirts and pants covered the bags. Paul was thankful for the fortification; it broke the sharpness of the cutting wind. He could not imagine how those who did not have the supplementary insulation would be able to survive the brutal weather, especially on days like today.

No one knew what the commotion was about that morning, but there was a definite uneasiness among the prisoners, and whispered speculations that they were going to be executed. Most were nearly dead already; some had died in the bunks during the night. They had succumbed to the usual "natural" killers: disease, starvation, and exhaustion. The rest barely had the strength to stand upright in the cold. They huddled close together, hoping to absorb any heat that might radiate from their neighbor's body. The bones of their skeletal structures protruded sharply, pressing into each other.

Finally the order came.

"Stay together! We are evacuating the camp. Anyone who tries to escape will be shot."

"*Ma Nishtanah?*"[37] A sea of about 3,000 starving, emaciated prisoners set out on foot in what felt to be below-zero temperatures. For the amount of protection their clothing afforded, they might as well have worn nothing. The unrelenting wind ripped through the light fabric, instantly chilling their bodies to the bone. Men and women shivered violently as, by sheer will, they forced one foot in front of the other, pace after pace, shuffle after shuffle, for endless miles. The soles of wet, frozen feet burned with each step on the icy road. Their faces froze in expressionless masks, the wind pounding and drying their eyes. They squinted, trying in vain to minimize the sting. Chins were drawn to the chest and arms crossed tightly over the heart, as all remaining survival instincts were summoned to conserve and sustain what little body heat they had for as long as possible.

Supervising them, in staggered, irregular formation, were German SS officers. They walked along each side of the crowded road, keeping the massive group in relative order. These guards were not particularly anxious to murder prisoners; they simply wanted to reach their destination — Gross Rosen — as quickly as possible. Stationed at the rear of the group were a handful of the notorious SS killing commandos. They wore several layers of warm clothing, sturdy leather boots and gloves, and thick full-length leather coats. They were armed with automatic handguns and eager to shoot anyone

---

[37] *Ma Nishtanah* — (pro. Mah NEESH-tah-NAH) reference to a traditional question asked by Jewish children on the night of Passover: "Why is this night different from all other nights?" Used in context here as a sarcastic slang.

63

who moved outside of the ranks or who could not keep up with the marching column.

Almost immediately, the weakened bodies of prisoners yielded to the elements. To drop from exhaustion meant death — either from the cold or from an SS bullet. The first gunshot resonated through the frigid air when the first man fell. Warm crimson blood mingled with newly fallen snow, causing a waft of steam to rise from the spot. Someone began to whisper words from the Torah: "The soul of the flesh is in the blood"[38] and continued with the Mourner's Kaddish: "*Yis Gadal V'Yis Kadash Sh'may Rabah* . . ."[39] No one stopped walking.

After that, every mile saw dozens of people fall. They had neither the strength nor the endurance to continue in the cold. Accompanying each fall was the piercing crack of gunfire. The fatal shot was always delivered to the back of the head — it guaranteed death. Hundreds died that day. Corpses lined the sides of the road, leaving a trail of Jewish blood on German soil. Even so, the human mass continued to move incessantly forward. Whenever they were able to conjure the strength to bend over without falling, prisoners scooped handfuls of snow. For a few seconds at a time, it helped to relieve thirst and the excruciating pain of an empty stomach.

Arriving at a small town, one of the SS guards called Paul to him. He was not one of the commando killers, but Paul felt anxious just the same.

"We're coming into a town," the officer told him. "Run fast into one of the stores and grab as much food as you can. Get out quickly. Come here — I'll tell you where and when to go." Paul tried to assess the officer's expression. Was he serious or was this a setup? The SS did not need an excuse to kill prisoners, so if he wanted to kill him, why didn't he just do it? The man looked genuinely at Paul. There seemed to be a sobriety, even a kind of sadness, or perhaps regret, in his eyes.

Periodically in his years in the concentration camps, Paul had observed this phenomenon in some of the officers. It was a rarity in the SS, but there

---

[38] From the third book of the Bible, Leviticus 17:11.

[39] Mourner's *Kaddish* — (pro. KAH-dish) Often mistaken as a "prayer for the dead," the Kaddish is an ancient Hebrew prayer of praise and thanks to God. It is recited or canted at the death (or memorial commemoration of the death) of a loved one.

64

were those who never seemed to have acquired the appetite for killing. He spoke quietly to him in German. "You want me to steal food?" The officer nodded his head. "Yes. You're strong and fast. Take as much as you can get."

He had observed something different about Paul — something that made him stand out in the crowd. He was not quite as emaciated as the other prisoners were. His body had not yet entirely wasted away from food deprivation; he still had a minimal amount of musculature beneath his skin. The officer did not know why, nor did he seem to care. His only concern was that Paul appeared to be stronger and more able to accomplish this feat than anyone else in the crowd. Paul, however, knew the reason for his strength: Hans had taken exceptional care of his would-be son. He had faithfully provided him with extra portions of nutritious food and necessary medical treatment for the duration of his incarceration at Blechhammer. Because of that care, Paul had been able to maintain nominal body mass and vitality.

As they approached one of the stores, the man placed his hand on Paul's shoulder. "Go!" he urged him, pushing him in the direction of a lighted doorway. Paul ran into the store. The store's merchant stood in the presence of the hungry thief. Paul hesitated for a moment when their eyes met, but his focus quickly turned to the food. All around them, suspended from the ceiling and hanging in the store's window, were smoked sausages. On the tables and countertops were dozens of loaves of freshly baked bread. He reached for them, the bread first and then the sausages. Snatching all that he could hold in his arms, he turned once more to look at the merchant. The man did not move, yell, or try to restrain him.

Paul turned toward the door, ran back to the officer, and handed him the goods. With haste, the officer removed a knife from his belt and began slicing the food. Paul wondered if this Nazi could possibly know what real hunger was. He turned his face away, disgusted by the prospect of the officer's self-indulgence. Within the next few seconds, however, the sausage and bread were being distributed to the starving prisoners around him. Puzzled, Paul turned back and looked up at the man. He handed a generous share to his young accomplice. Paul thought that he had retrieved the food for the SS guards — it had never occurred to him that a Nazi would ever feed prisoners.

65

This was unheard of . . . an SS officer with *rachmunus?*[40] Paul did not know what to make of this display of kindness. He had never witnessed mercy from the SS; it simply didn't fit the profile.

His father's last words came to mind. "God will look after you." He could not help but think that the words must indeed be true. Someone must be looking after him. How else could all of this be explained? He recalled the care he had been shown over the past five years and wondered if perhaps heaven housed a new guardian and his father was taking care of him from above. Why else would an SS officer try to help him . . . or any Jews at all? As he walked in the snow and wind, he contemplated the lot that providence may have cast on his family. He tried not to imagine the worst, yet the worst was all he was able to imagine. He wanted to cry. He couldn't. There were no tears left. Instead, he looked to the sky and made a *bruchah*[41] for the generous provision of the day.

The reflection of the snow-covered earth created a dusky glow in the twilight sky. The dwindling assembly continued to walk throughout the day and into the evening until, finally, daylight gave way to night. Their clothing was drenched from falling snow, and their battered feet could barely sustain the weight of their slight frames. They were too tired, too weak, and too sick to think about escaping. They had nowhere to run. Besides, perhaps by some miracle they might survive this war after all. A few optimistic souls still believed that as long as there was life, there was hope.

They moved off the main road and took shelter wherever they were able to find it. Some were fortunate enough to seize a piece of accommodating ground in roadside barns; others lay under trees, bushes, or anywhere they were able to find cover. Those who had endured the day could think of nothing but sleep. In this moment, even thoughts of their loved ones — of spouses, parents, and children for whom they so desperately yearned — were absent from their consciousness. Sleep. The group lay on the hard, frozen ground, flocking together in a massive cluster, shivering in damp clothes under the unrelenting bitter wind. Many would not awaken with the rising sun.

---

[40] *Rachmunus* — (Hebrew/Yiddish, pro. rokh-MOO-nuhs) tender mercy or compassion.
[41] *Bruchah* — (pro. BRUH-khuh) a blessing.

They marched for a week, each day's toll of bodies surpassing that of the previous one. By day, they walked along frigid roads. By night, when fortune smiled on them, they slept in barns hoping against hope to wake in the morning. With each passing town and village, the officer sent Paul to retrieve food. The procedure was always the same: The officer chose the store; Paul made the conquest. Most of the merchants lived in apartments behind their stores and came out of their living quarters only when a bell on the door rang, alerting them to a customer's entrance. Paul became such an ace in the art of stealing groceries that he was in and out of the store before the owner even had a chance to get there. The food he took was always divided among prisoners by the hand of the perplexing goodwill officer. It was an unlikely partnership, Paul and an SS Nazi. But it worked, and at least a few people were kept alive by the provisions. This Nazi was an enigma and a paradox, but then again, everything about the war seemed a paradox. It was useless to try to analyze it logically.

The weather grew even fiercer, claiming more lives, and imposing more suffering. Paul walked along the outside edge of the group, holding his head low, his arms wrapped tightly around his upper body. Still, the wind battered his flesh. He was thankful to have the cement bag underneath his clothing. Although the layers of paper insulation were just enough to keep his vital organs alive, they did not provide adequate essential warmth. He didn't think he would be able to endure much more of the cold. He closed his eyes for a few moments at a time as he trudged through the snow. The combined effects of sleep deprivation, physical exhaustion, hunger, thirst, and the stinging wind were too much. He wanted to lie down and sleep. Everyone wanted to lie down and sleep. Many had already succumbed to hypothermia and did lie down to sleep. They never got up.

Keep moving. Along the edge of the road was a hill leading down to a ravine. Running through the ravine was a frozen creek. Overcome by exhaustion, Paul miscalculated a step and tumbled down the hill. He hit hard on the surface of the creek, breaking the ice and falling into the frigid water. Immediately, he was immersed. Survival instincts took over and he somehow managed to pull himself out. He could barely breathe; he felt as though his

67

lungs had been paralyzed. He pushed himself to his feet and climbed back up the hill. He was soaked through to his flesh, dripping for a few moments until every layer of clothing and paper insulation froze to a solid against his tender skin. Someone came up from behind, pushing him off the main road toward a woodsy area. The voice was German.

"Come with me." It was the SS officer. Paul was terrified. He knew what was in store for prisoners who could no longer continue on the march.

"Please don't kill me," Paul pleaded. He imagined what a bullet to the brain might feel like. "Please, don't kill me," he pleaded again. He thought of his father.

"Shh. Don't talk. Take off your clothes and put this on." The officer handed him a sweater.

"Are you going to kill me?"

"No, I am not going to kill you. Put these clothes on now." Paul struggled to remove his frozen clothes and the underlying cement bag. His body was shaking uncontrollably. The officer helped him pull the sweater over his head and onto his torso. Promptly, he removed his own leather coat, tore off the Nazi insignia, and pulled it over Paul's arms. He wrapped and buttoned the coat around the boy's chest. It still held the warmth from his body. In a few minutes, Paul stopped shivering. Beyond them, on the road, more gunshots rang out.

"Put your clothes on over the coat. Hurry," the officer urged.

"What about you?" Paul asked.

"I have another one. Just worry about yourself."

Paul pulled the wet clothing over the coat. He stood upright and the two turned toward the road. Together, they walked out of the trees and rejoined the march.

Weimar / Buchenwald

By the time they reached Gross Rosen, many of the prisoners were dead. Those who had survived the march stayed in barracks, waiting to be transferred to Buchenwald, a notorious concentration camp near Weimar, Germany. What limited food resources had been available were now depleted even further, and the majority of other supplies and equipment had been decimated in warfare. The German criminals who ran Gross Rosen were merciless in their beatings, often inflicting fatal injuries to prisoners.

There was nothing to be done. The people simply waited for the next chapter of the nightmare. It came a week later.

Starving prisoners were given a piece of bread and loaded onto a train. The rail cars were open-topped coal cars; the walls stood about five feet high. For three days, they traveled in below-freezing temperatures, once again fully exposed to the bitterly cold air. When they finally arrived in Weimar on February 10, 1945, they were significantly fewer in number than at the outset three days prior.

Weimar was renowned for its natural beauty and for its prestigious university. Nestled in a valley at the base of sprawling mountains, the town was the picture of German pride. The university accorded its residents a reputation of class, distinction, and intelligence. It was a tragic irony that in the midst of such exalted thinking, such indifference to human suffering could exist. As endless trainloads of starving and dying people were systematically delivered to their town, the residents of Weimar chose to look the other way.

Buchenwald was hidden in the oak woods on Ettersberg Mountain, only a few kilometers outside and north of the city. The prisoners were to be transported as soon as military trains departed the depot. The railway stations acted as repositories for artillery stored onsite in makeshift warehouses. Military trains that had survived the war came through to pick up and deliver the artillery to areas in the country where the battered German army continued to fight its final battles.

The prisoners waited, huddled together, shivering in the open boxcars, the mist of their breath crystallizing in the winter air. Patches of frostbitten skin and white, frozen appendages had become commonplace. They were silent. They no longer possessed the strength to speak. There was nothing to speak about. In the stillness, they awaited their fate like corpses awaiting interment.

The sudden rumble of distant plane engines drew everyone's eyes to the sky. Trapped inside the boxcars, the helpless prisoners could do nothing but watch as American bombers approached.[42] The pilots were unaware of the caged innocent people beneath their planes. The bombs began to fall, exploding on and around the train amid terrified shrieks. The blast of stored artillery in nearby trains and warehouses sent debris flying everywhere. Shrapnel and other trajectories were hurled with tremendous explosive force through the train cars. Chaos ensued as people fell en masse, blood covering the bodies of the living and the dead.

Paul leapt toward the side of the train. He pulled himself over the wall and jumped onto the pavement below. He scurried onto the tracks under the train, covering his head as the car above him convulsed with the pounding and skewering of flying objects. The explosions continued for only a short while, but the devastation was enormous. When he emerged, he was surrounded by dead and dying people. The train that, only minutes earlier, had borne the barely living, now held piles of body parts and vacant human shells.

The tracks had been destroyed in the bombing. The surviving prisoners would have to make the mountainous trek to the concentration camp on foot. Less than ten miles away, another camp — Dora-Mittelbau (originally a sub-camp of Buchenwald that later became its own camp) — was a place of extermination for thousands of prisoners. Few came out of there alive. Dense black smoke billowed night and day from its chimneys as Nazis scrambled to destroy the evidence of their abomination. Hundreds of prisoners were "processed" every hour. The gray ash of their burned remains covered the snow.

● ● ●

When the prisoners from Blechhammer and Gross Rosen arrived at Buchenwald, only a fraction of the original number remained. Some had been mortally wounded on the train and were unable to endure the difficult mountain terrain; some had succumbed to starvation or exhaustion, or had suffered frozen extremities in which gangrene had quickly set in; some simply no longer possessed the will to live. Those who were unable to continue

---

[42] The Americans targeted the German railway stations to destroy both their artillery storehouses and whatever remained of their transportation system.

70

moving up the mountain were shot by SS guards. The mountain path from Weimar to Buchenwald was littered with bodies. All of Germany and Poland, in fact, were littered with the dead, their skies polluted with the ash and their soil with the blood of millions of Jews.

Formed in 1937 as a political prison camp, Buchenwald was transformed into a huge concentration camp in the early 1940s. Scores of thousands of foreign slave laborers were crammed into the camp as it became a central institution in the far-flung SS slave labor industrial empire. Buchenwald was the Grand Central Station, a trans-shipping place to numerous sub-camps, including Dora, Madeburg, Zeitz, and others.

The camp was surrounded by barbed wire. It seemed a ridiculous formality at this point. Where were they to go? They were on a snow-covered mountain surrounded by forests in the middle of nowhere; no food, no water, no clothing, no provisions, no strength. Most were barely able to walk or speak.

But, at Buchenwald, to the surprise of the Death March survivors, the German Communist-led international underground — along with Czech, French, and Russian allies — seemed influential in the administration of the camp. Prisoners were hopeful as they were processed into the large cinema building, being assigned new clothing and prisoner registration numbers.

Every segment of Paul's frozen body ached as he and the group once again moved steadily forward in protracted lines. He mentally enlisted all reserves of will and strength to fight the urge to collapse. Remain vertical. Do NOT buckle. Finally, his moment had arrived. He stood in front of a Czech guard and was registered as prisoner number 126259. The numbers, vocalized in the guard's native tongue, echoed in Paul's brain . . . *jeden dva sest dva pet devet . . . jeden dva sest dva pet devet . . . jeden dva sest dva pet devet . . .*

The German communists had organized a rescue operation to protect the throngs of incoming children. Teenagers and younger children were segregated during processing and taken to a remote barrack, block 66, a distance from the main camp. There, nearly 1,000 children were cared for by the resistance. To a large extent, the SS remained uninvolved.

71

For Paul, however, fate was not so kind. Where lying about his age in preceding camps had saved his life, this time it would consign the adolescent boy to a place of grave danger. Because his documented age was nineteen rather than his actual age of fourteen, he was placed in the Kleinelager — the lower camp — in barrack 52 where most adult newcomers were assigned. Of all the barracks of Buchenwald, this was the most vile and notorious. Down in the festering "little camp," Block 52 was filled to capacity and large transports like this one pushed the camp toward overcrowding. Cadavers were stacked outside the barracks, waiting to be carted away to the crematoria.

Exhausted, frozen, and starving, the newest arrivals took their places on the hard wooden slabs — five or six emaciated veteran prisoners to each five-foot width of barrack bunk. They slept pressed tightly together, their bodies providing the only limited warmth in the cold winter air.

Masses of incoming prisoners flooded Buchenwald. There was no room to accommodate the continuous influx. More than ten thousand prisoners had arrived from Auschwitz and its evacuated sub-camps — Buna, Blechhammer, Jawosowice, and others — from late January to mid-February. Something had to be done.

Inmates were called from the barracks, given a loaf of bread, and told they were to be transported to another location to work in one of the Buchenwald sub-camps. Transports to the outer camps continued through February and March of 1945, where prisoners were put to work making gasoline and armaments, building bunkers, and transferring goods. Those who became ill or diseased were brought back to Buchenwald and disposed of there. Others were shunted around in the constellation of 120-some camps that reported to the Buchenwald command.

During the two months Paul was there, each day was marked by the excruciating pain of hunger. As the Allied bombing campaign disrupted the already limited flow of supplies to the camp, prisoners went for long periods without eating. When they received food, it was very small rations of stale bread made with sawdust in place of flour. Most of the prisoners consumed their bread immediately. Some saved it for the morning, guarding it through the night from would-be thieves by sleeping on top of it. When they were awake, thoughts of food dominated their minds. When they slept, the same

72

thoughts infiltrated their dreams. When spring arrived and the earth warmed, prisoners dug in the dirt for insects, grubs, and worms, which provided a little protein. After a while, though, even the earth refused its yield; the highly coveted earthworms had all been harvested.

For a while, thick, dark smoke continued to rise from the chimneys of the crematoria night and day. Near the end, though, fuel to run the ovens ran out, as the Allied Forces thoroughly and methodically destroyed Germany's resources. Bodies lay strewn about in the streets or were thrown onto mounded piles throughout the lower camp. The decaying cadavers served as a constant reminder to inmates of their imminent fate. Lacking any semblance of humanness — any evidence of having once been breathing, living, loving souls — the corpses now existed only as a part of the landscape. A festering testament to the inconceivable, they were no longer who, but what.

During the final days, the Nazis sought to round up Jewish (and other) inmates to take them on marches. Most prisoners knew what was happening when the call for all the Jews to line up on the *appellplatz* (a central area for roll call) was sounded late in the afternoon of April 4. They resisted, failing to assemble. Among them was not-yet-fifteen-year-old Paul. The Nazis subsequently used bread to lure the starving prisoners in the little camp out of the buildings, barrack by barrack. Paul knew what they were up to. For four years, he had witnessed their trickery, manipulation, and barbarism. He was not about to fall for it. He and a few others took the bread and ran back into the barrack. The rest of the prisoners in the cluster were taken into the woods and shot.

Within a few days of the incident, Paul became critically ill and lost his ability to walk. He was carried to the camp hospital where he was admitted for "evaluation." Evaluation in this place consisted of a syringe full of cyanide. A German communist *kapo* approached him in his bed. He had received information that Paul was scheduled for execution that week, and was determined to help. He looked down upon the young patient.

"I don't want you to worry, son. I am going to make sure nothing happens to you while you're in here. I'll take care of you."

The elder held to his word and protected Paul for the duration of his stay. He knew Paul was only a child, but was powerless to transfer (or even smuggle) him to the children's block. There was no room to operate outside of the ever-watchful eye of the SS . . . at least not in that capacity. He kept Paul in the infirmary longer than what was necessary for his recovery. In this way, the scheduled day of Paul's execution passed, and he returned safely to his barrack. His execution was rescheduled for April 20— Adolph Hitler's birthday.

When Paul returned to block 52, hushed rumors circulated through the bunks: some of the men were surviving by consuming the decaying flesh of the cadavers. A fellow prisoner came to Paul. He concealed something in his hand; from what Paul was able to see, it looked to be red.

"What do you have?" he asked the man.

"Eat this. It will keep you alive." The starving man handed Paul a piece of raw meat. He was reluctant to take it.

"What is it? Where did you get this?"

The man sank his rotting teeth into the flesh, pulled off a small piece, and swallowed. "You want to live? Just eat it. Don't ask questions." Paul ate the meat. He didn't have to ask again, nor did he want to. ✡

CHAPTER 5

Liberation

The date was April 11, 1945. The few hundred remaining inmates at Buchenwald had resigned themselves to death. They waited for it — for the liberation it would bring — without a thought, without a fight, without even a prayer. Lines of sunken eyes in barely living, barely breathing, casing-covered skeletons lay still and silent on the wooden slabs. The barracks were quiet . . . very quiet.

Like everyone around him, Paul was dying. His organs had begun to fail, causing fluid to accumulate under his skin. The edema obscured the gravity of his condition — swelling had filled in spaces on his body that would otherwise have appeared to be nothing more than membranes and bone. He lay prone and listless on the bunk, a nonentity devoid of conscious thought, devoid of anything that might define life. An occasional fleeting picture of his family, the involuntary firing of neurons, was all that connected him to his once human life. He turned his face to his left arm. Number 176520. He closed his eyes.

A loud shot rang outside, violating the stillness. It meant nothing; it was a sound so familiar, it no longer elicited even the slightest reaction. A few seconds later another shot sounded, then another, and another until their ears could no longer distinguish individual shots in a barrage of firing. It was not the routine sound of mass executions. Something different was happening today. They sat up, looking to each other for answers. It was the first real sign of life they had exhibited in weeks. A thunderous explosion sent some of the men to their feet.

"What's happening?" they cried, not really expecting a response.

"This is it. We're all going to die." Someone's words reverberated through the air, lacking the emotional tenor that would normally accompany such a statement. The words lingered for a moment before driving the men from the bunks. More explosions, more shots, and piercing, unfamiliar noises sparked life in the dying.

75

They moved as quickly toward the door as their failing bodies would allow. Outside, watchtowers exploded into flames and tumbled to the ground, sending the SS guards and their machine guns flying through the air. Other guards panicked and threw down their guns, running in no particular direction to seek cover. But there was no refuge for them. Everywhere, grenades, bullets, and explosive artillery found them.

"They're being shot!" prisoners shouted. "Someone is shooting the guards!" Nazis rushed the barracks, pushing the frail men out of their way as they ripped their SS uniforms from their bodies. In a frantic attempt to disguise their identity, they snatched the standard issue of inmate clothing and covered their naked forms. A supernatural wave of strength infused the prisoners, granting them rebirth into life. They retrieved the discarded SS pistols from the ground and began to shoot the guards.

Outside, the frenzy continued. Where only ten minutes before there had been deathly silence, a wall of deafening noise reverberated.

"What's going on?" Paul demanded an answer.

"The Yankees are here!" someone yelled. "The Yanks are breaking through the fence! Look for yourself!"

Khaki green tanks, each emblazoned with a white five-pointed star, an American flag, and decals proudly displaying the letters *U.S.A.* plowed through the once impenetrable barrier of barbed wire fencing. Within minutes, the camp's yard was teeming with the foreign liberators. They came in tanks and on foot, blasting everything in their path.

"Are we going to die? What's going on? Who are the Yanks?" A rush of excitement filled Paul's senses. He didn't know where to look or what to watch. Guards were being shot by soldiers and prisoners alike, buildings were exploding, and chaos engulfed the camp.

The American liberators were horrified at what they found. Rumors of atrocities had circulated among their troops, but no one would have believed the extent of Nazi savagery without witnessing it firsthand. Even the soldiers who had fought in the bloodiest battles of the war had never seen anything of this magnitude. The stench of hundreds of rotting bodies drove them to cover their noses and mouths. Corpses were stacked like logs in some areas of the camp; others were piled in mounds or scattered indiscriminately on the

76

grounds. Thousands were found decaying in the woods beyond the fence, where they had been shot en masse but were too numerous to bury. The crematorium had been operating day and night for months but could not keep up with the demand.

The Americans rounded up SS guards by the dozens. Those who attempted to conceal their status were easily identified, not only by their healthy appearance, but also by the tattoos under their left arms.

With liberation came ad hoc justice. Some guards were detained to be used later in forced labor; others were turned over to inmates. There was no mercy for the guilty. A notorious SS murderer, a sadistic guard who tortured and killed a minimum of ten people every day, now found himself in the custody of two prisoners.

"I'm innocent! I'm innocent!" he screamed repeatedly as his captors pinned him to the ground, enlisting the help of a large pointed shovel to exact their revenge.

The thrust of the war shifted as victim now assumed the role of executioner — no trial required. None of the SS officers were spared.

Prisoners looked in awe at the dense smoke rising from the burning buildings. Only a few hours earlier, the terrible stench of a different black smoke had darkened the sky. An image of unspeakable depravity, it had billowed from the camp for what seemed to be an eternity. Now a new smoke rose. This was not a byproduct of fire and human flesh, but rather the fiery banner of liberation. The evil that for too long had imposed such an abomination upon humanity was finally ending.

● ● ●

The Americans quickly restored order by sending prisoners back to the barracks. When the commotion receded, an announcement resonated in German over the camp's intercom.

"Please return to the bunks! Food and medication will be brought to you." Food was rapidly transported into the camp and distributed among the starving prisoners. "There is enough for everyone. You may have as much as you like." The benevolent strangers aided the former prisoners in spooning food into their bowls. Indeed, there appeared to be no limit not only to

77

the quantity, but also to the variety of foods. There was meat, soup, bread, vegetables, fruits — it was endless. It was Utopia. Not since the years prior to their incarceration had these men seen such an abundance of food. Paul had *never* witnessed such plenty; it was difficult to fathom. There were foods that he didn't even know existed — foods like white bread . . . prepared without sawdust.

Prisoners were overcome with emotion. Primal instinct drove them to devour everything within their grasp, but their physical condition remained extremely grave. Soldiers were quickly instructed to distribute the food slowly for the welfare and safety of the dying people. At this stage of starvation, eating too much too quickly could kill them.

"Here, take this." One of the Americans handed Paul a pill. He supported his head with one hand and held a glass of water with the other as Paul swallowed.

"This boy is so weak, he can barely move," the soldier said quietly to the attending physician. Paul's head and hands trembled. The doctor came near and pulled his lower eyelids down, revealing the tender underlying flesh. After a few moments of examination, he said to an interpreter, "Tell this kid we're going to take care of him and that he's going to be okay. Tell him he'll be just fine." The doctor nodded and smiled at Paul as the interpreter spoke the words in German.

Who *are* these Yankees? Paul could not understand why the Americans would travel across the Atlantic Ocean to rescue them. In his three and a half years of schooling, he had learned very little about life outside of Poland. He was mystified by the power, the compassion, and the generosity of the "Yankee soldiers." Heaven must have sent them, he thought.

After the liberation of the camp, Paul stayed in Buchenwald for another two weeks. The Americans continued to care for him and the other prisoners until their health returned. They provided a constant supply of medication, food, and support. Being only fourteen years old, Paul's move toward recovery was swift. As soon as he was able to get around on his own, he headed out from the camp. Walking with nothing more than the thin, tattered prison uniform on his back and a few rations of food, he set his face toward the East. He would return to Bielsko to begin searching for his family.

The Search

It was more than four hundred miles from Weimar to Bielsko. Paul began the long trek toward his home on the Autobahn, the same highway that had demanded his sweat and labor just a few years before. Though the war had ended, the ironies had not. He thought about the people who had been buried — dead and alive — under the very concrete on which he now walked. This ground had become the eternal resting place of countless souls. A place that ought to have been revered as a memorial for the dead, it was now a surface for thousands of trucks and automobiles to make their way from one place to another. Paul stopped and watched, tears filling his eyes. The souls of mothers, fathers, and their babies cried out to him. The irreverence of the sight was unthinkable.

The world looked different from the outside, but a lingering sense of the camps governed his spirit. The more he attempted to rid himself of the morbid sensations and impressions, the more they gnawed at him. He moved forward with other frail but determined prisoners, still clothed in striped uniforms, as they trudged slowly along the sides of the busy highway toward their distant homes. Some walked alone, some in pairs or small groups.

Many headed south toward Hof an der Saale[43] near the Bavarian border. Hitler was dead — he had committed suicide by cyanide and gunshot in a bunker in Berlin when defeat was imminent — and the new leadership in the German government stepped in to start aiding the war refugees. There, in the American Zone,[44] the city of Hof provided a place of lodging for thousands of weary displaced people.

While on the superhighway, Paul met a German man who had been liberated from a death camp. The identification label on his uniform indicated that he was a Communist. The Nazis despised Communists almost as

---

[43] Hof an der Saale (pro. hohf ahn der TZAH-luh) Hof is a city on the Saale River in Bavaria, West Germany. During the period immediately following the war, it was considered part of the American-occupied territory.

[44] In addition to the American Zone, there were also Russian, British, and French zones. The American-, French-, and British-occupied territories in Western Europe provided protection, shelter, and aid to the Jewish refugees. In contrast, the Russian-occupied areas tolerated anti-Semitic activity, allowing Polish and German vigilantes to continue killing Jews.

79

much as they did Jews. He was a dissident, and therefore an enemy, deemed unworthy to share the same breathing space as the elite. He and Paul walked together for many long miles, exchanging stories about their experiences in the camps, their lives before the war, and their families. Paul explained that he planned to travel through Saxony, Germany. It was located just east of them and was on the way to Poland. He hoped to receive word of his family there.

Paul was extremely thin and weak. The transitional time he spent at Buchenwald after his liberation resurrected him into the world of the living but did little to rebuild his vigor. After traveling on foot for many miles, Paul and his new acquaintance were exhausted. Eventually they hitched a ride with American GIs. The soldiers fed them and took them as far as Saxony. Paul was grateful for the food and for the ride, but more than anything, he was grateful for his freedom. He still could not believe what had happened to him. It must be a dream, he thought. His childhood had been stolen, but he was alive and he was free. God willing, so was his family. He was determined to find them. It was all that mattered to him now.

Paul and his companion stopped at a farm in Crimmitschau.[45] A middle-aged German couple who had lost their sons in the war welcomed the weary travelers into their home. The young Communist stayed with the farmers for only a few days before continuing on his way. Paul stayed for several weeks. They were kind and generous people, extending not only hospitality to the teenager, but also the sorrow-laden love of brokenhearted parents. He became their prince by proxy, the object of vicarious adoration. They treated him like a son, a young man who had come home to them when their own sons could not. He ate the finest food, slept in a warm, soft bed, and enjoyed (for the first time in five years) the comfort and nurturing of a loving home. Something about Paul, perhaps his boyish vulnerability, helped to ease the suffering of their loss. This was not the first time he had that effect on grieving people. He had been taken under the wing of a surrogate parent once before. He wondered what had become of Hans.

Paul's strength returned slowly but steadily, and he wasted no time in resuming his search. He frequented Crimmitschau's downtown area where

---

[45] Crimmitschau (pro. KRIH-mih-chow) a small town in Saxony, West Germany.

80

he befriended the *Beurgermeister*.[46] The man was a decent soul and took a special interest in Paul. He supplied him with clothing, leather boots, a full-length leather coat, and even a motorcycle — all remnant Nazi gear. He sympathized with Paul's plight and offered to help in whatever way he was able. He suggested that Paul visit the American 76th Infantry Division. The combat soldiers of the unit had built a refugee camp where there was a constant influx of displaced survivors of the war. Perhaps he might find his family there or at least receive news of them.

Paul made his way through town to the camp, inquiring as he went. Arriving at the unit, he tried to enlist the aid of army personnel. Unfortunately, no one was able to help him; there was no record of anyone in his family.

"Keep coming back, kid. Keep checking. There are more people coming in every day, and they're coming from all around," they said, encouraging him.

Though frustrating, the time he spent in Crimmitschau was not wasted. Over the next several weeks, Paul returned to the unit headquarters on a regular basis. As he continued to search, he developed friendships with the Americans. One of his new friends was a high-ranking officer in the Red Cross division. "It's like trying to find a needle in a haystack, Paul," the man told him. "There are millions of people missing . . . millions. Can you understand? I don't know if you'll *ever* find your family, but we'll keep our eyes and ears open for you." Paul was painfully aware of the prospect of being separated from his family forever. Hearing the words spoken by a man in this position, however, solidified the tragedy in a way that he had not yet allowed himself to consider.

With increasing frustration came rage. Paul had witnessed such extreme brutality for so long, the normal boundaries of right and wrong had blurred. Taken from his home as a child, he had grown into manhood under the most deplorable conditions. Torture, murder, violence, hatred — these were the common threads of his adolescent experience. He lacked the coping mechanisms common to most adults and was immersed in a culvert of unprocessed emotional trauma. There was no place to relegate the horrors and no means of escape. Instead, the atrocities hung before him, suspended in the

---

[46] *Beurgermeister* — (German, pro. BUHR-geh-mei-ster) town chairman or mayor.

81

forefront of his thoughts: flashes of screaming children, hangings, beatings, smoke rising from immense brick chimneys, and everywhere, blood. Blood on dirt, blood on walls, blood on snow.

Liberation was not freedom after all. Paul was liberated in body, yet his spirit remained captive. With each passing day, fury became a demon companion. Escalating anguish possessed him like a fever, mounting higher day after day, until he knew what he must do. He must have revenge.

He purchased a knife from a small shop in town. The weapon had been crafted in such a way that it was perfectly balanced. The weight, design, and materials ensured its accuracy when thrown. Provided the aim was decent, the point would always find its target. He couldn't miss. Paul placed it in a sheath and tucked it into one of the tall leather Nazi boots he now wore. The readiness of his weapon was ever on his mind as he waited to use it.

● ● ●

Spring was nearly spent. Most of Paul's time had been devoted to the search for his family, and despite his intense focus on vengeance, Paul's amiable personality proved his greatest asset. Several people in the American unit had developed a fondness for the gregarious and persistent boy. They were actively involved on his behalf, checking and double-checking the identities of refugees, just in case an Argiewicz or Schwartzfochs might materialize.

Paul developed an especially close relationship with a Jewish American chaplain of the unit named Ziemack. There was an instant kinship, and they spent many hours together, forming what would later become a critical alliance. Ziemack kept close tabs on Paul and gave him generous quantities of food, clothing, and other necessities.

It seemed that everywhere Paul turned, someone was taking care of him. In between trips to town, he continued to recuperate on the farm. He circled around populated neighborhoods and the sprawling German countryside on his new *Gestapo* motorcycle. Enjoying the luxury of freedom, he scoured the area for information on his family. He sought out residents and refugees alike, asking questions and describing his loved ones. Surely, there

82

is someone who knows something, he thought. No one did. Everyone was busy looking for their own fathers, mothers, siblings, and children.

When the rains came, he abandoned the motorcycle in favor of a small car, compliments of the *Beurgermeister.* Because gasoline was scarce and expensive, he bummed it off American GIs. They always carried an extra five-gallon tank of gas on the back of their jeeps and were all too happy to oblige "the kid with the car." They, like so many others, were amused by the teenager's tenacity.

Eventually, the time came for Paul to leave Crimmitschau. The chaplain informed him that the American combat division would soon be moving to Hof. The Allied Forces had recently signed a treaty that granted Russia control of the eastern half of Germany, all of Czechoslovakia, Poland, and the other eastern European countries. The Americans, British, and French, in turn, had been given control of the West. Saxony was in the eastern section of Germany, and the Russians would be moving in very soon. The combat soldiers of the 76th Infantry Division were to relinquish control of the area immediately. Ziemack explained to Paul that it could become dangerous for him to stay in that area. Turbulent times were ahead for the East. He should consider following the Americans to Bavaria rather than returning to Poland. Paul agreed to drive to Hof as soon as he had gathered his things and bid his hosts farewell.

It was time to move on anyway. Several weeks had passed, and his search had been unsuccessful. Perhaps he would have better luck in Hof. After all, most of the refugees would be transferred from Eastern Europe to the West. It only made sense that his chances of finding his family would increase if he looked for them there. He was sure it was the right move. A sense of excitement filled him as he anticipated the prospect. It was short-lived. Doubt finagled its way into his mind, taunting him with thoughts of the inevitable. Would he find them healthy? Unchanged? Would he find them at all?

Paul spent his last night in Saxony with the German farmers. They ate, talked, and exchanged words of mutual affection. He would miss them, and they him. He knew he could never thank them adequately for all they had done on his behalf. How could he even begin to express his gratitude?

He gathered his few belongings the next morning, kissed them goodbye, and drove away from the lavender sunrise.

• • •

Paul found Hof to be more chaotic than Crimmitschau. Concentration camp survivors flocked into the city by the thousands. They came from East Germany, Poland, Russia, and Czechoslovakia. The Americans provided care for the homeless, and a large local tavern served as a place of shelter. Everywhere, refugees searched for their lost loved ones.

Paul camped in the tavern for just a short while. He combed the cot-filled room, scanning hundreds of faces, but doubted that he would be so lucky as to stumble on any of his family so soon. He was right. He found his way to the American headquarters, where Ziemack greeted him and showed him to his office inside the building. He shared it with the Red Cross administrator. Paul was content to be reunited with his friends. They took him with them every day to eat in the kitchen on the base. Ziemack explained to the cook that the boy was a concentration camp survivor, and the man gave him extra-large portions of food.

They also brought Paul along on their recreational excursions. They went frequently to a large soccer field in a nearby park where army personnel engaged in spirited team-sport competitions. Baseball was the favorite, and Ziemack, who stood well over six feet, shined among his teammates. It was Paul's first introduction to the game, and he enjoyed watching his friend play. When he learned the rules of the sport, he was even invited to join in the competition on occasion. Paul thought that America might not be a bad place to end up. If these people were any indication of what the rest of the population of the country was like, the U.S.A. would be a wonderful home. He certainly could not return to Poland, and given his experience in Germany, he would prefer to live elsewhere. From what he was told, America was open and welcoming to all people regardless of race, nationality, or religion. It sounded like Paradise on Earth, *Olam HaBa.*[47]

---

[47] *Olam HaBa* (Hebrew, pro. oh-LAHM hah-BAH) the world to come; the place of compensation for one's deeds after this life.

84

Although he was still only fifteen at the time, Paul took a job with the United Nations Relief and Rehabilitation Administration (UNRRA), driving a large open truck filled with supplies for refugees. In order to secure the position, he was compelled once again to lie about his age. The minimum age to drive a two-ton vehicle for the organization was twenty. This, however, did not really pose a problem for him since his identification card, issued by the American liberators of Buchenwald, recorded the year of his birth as 1926, rather than the actual 1930.[48] He had been taught as a child that it was wrong to lie, but lying had saved his life at the most critical times. If Paul had been honest with the Nazis, he would have been dead the day of his arrest at the *Durkankslager.* He did what he had to do to survive.

The job with UNRRA was good, and for the first time in his life, Paul was paid for his labor. On one end of the soccer field, the Americans stored hundreds of enormous boxes of food. The rations were covered with tarps to protect them from the elements. The quantity was staggering — Paul had never seen anything like it. There were cans of spam, meat, cheese, soups, oats, crackers. The bounty seemed to go on forever. There were also personal-care supplies and medications. He loaded the boxes in the truck and delivered them to the refugees. For every delivery he made, there was a stamped official order from the administration. His connection with UNRRA afforded him a constant supply of everything he needed. He lacked nothing — except what he desired most. He never stopped looking for his family, hoping against hope that on one of his deliveries, they would surface somewhere in the crowd.

Ziemack was able to convince some German residents in an apartment building next to the headquarters to take Paul in. It was too crowded and noisy in the tavern. He stayed with the Germans for a few weeks, scouring the area for familiar faces, and finally gave up. Nothing had materialized in Hof, and his sense of desperation was mounting. He heard that many young Jewish girls had found refuge in Japan and Russia. Perhaps he might find his

---

[48] In addition to the age discrepancy, Paul's identification card from Buchenwald also recorded his nationality as Polish. Although they lived in Poland, Jews generally were not regarded as "Polish," but rather simply as "Jewish." He did not volunteer this supplemental information to his liberators, as he feared his Jewish heritage would cause him to incur further prejudice and persecution as he ventured back into the world.

85

sister Lucy there. He would take his chances and travel east on the Trans-Siberian Railroad. It would be a dangerous journey, but fear held no sway for the survivors of the Nazi regime. What dangers could possibly lurk in the darkness that they had not already survived? Was there anything that could exceed the horrors they had endured?

Paul secured the knife in his boot and left the city. He turned his face toward another lavender sunrise, guided by his resolve to find Lucy. She was the only one of his family whose spirit he could still sense among the living. He prayed for help and set all his energies to finding her. He would gladly travel through the continent's ten time zones and even to the end of the earth to see her beautiful face again.

The Trans-Siberian Railroad

Paul hitchhiked through Germany. The journey afforded him copious opportunities to make new acquaintances. American GIs provided the majority of rides — they were always willing to give a lift. He liked the Americans. He found them to be friendly, generous people and he enjoyed learning the English language. Traveling through the Russian-occupied territories in a military vehicle posed a constant danger, though, so they did not drive him through those areas.

When Paul arrived in Sosnowiec, he inquired about his family. No one knew anything definitive, but the general consensus was that the Jews had all perished in Auschwitz and the other death camps. The Jewish ghetto had long since given up its Jews. The attitudes of many of the city's residents had remained unchanged. He found the Poles to be more anti-Semitic than ever, and now that the German occupation of Poland had ended, they were emboldened to reclaim what they had "lost." Not surprisingly, that included the homes, possessions, businesses, and properties of the Jews who had been dispersed and murdered. The Poles moved into vacated Jewish homes, making them their residences and casually claiming what did not belong to them.

Paul took a train from Sosnowiec to the Russian border and left Poland as quickly as he could. Once on the other side, he was able to leave the tension of the town behind and recalibrate his concentration. He sat at the station and waited for the train to appear. The distant sound of metal wheels clacking against the tracks brought him to his feet. An involuntary image of being crammed in a boxcar with sweating bony bodies crowded Paul's thoughts. The vision threatened to overpower him, but he defied it and pushed it from his mind. He was not going to think about that . . . not now . . . not today. Today was for Lucy. He listened for the train. The rumble of the coal-fueled steam engine grew stronger and louder until at last he could see the black smoke rising from the oncoming train. Against his will, his eyes were drawn to the smoke. He stood paralyzed as time stopped. The billowing dense black wisps propelled him back to the crematorium and into the horror of emaciated bodies, bones, and ash.

"No!" he exclaimed with a great effort, driving the vision from his mind. He regained his composure and went to stand by the tracks. He clutched his bag and inhaled deeply. He was ready.

Paul was in the company of Russian soldiers who were being transported to the Far East for their continuing war with Japan. When the train arrived in the station, he boarded it with the soldiers as if he were one of theirs. No one questioned him. The transport train was fully loaded with military equipment, personnel, food, and clothing supplies. It would go as far as Vladivostok on the Kamchatka Peninsula. From there, the soldiers would pick up other trains that would take them to China and Manchuria.

Paul settled in with the uniformed army recruits and immediately struck up conversation. He had learned some basic Russian in the camps, and his lack of fluency neither intimidated him nor dampened his eagerness to communicate with his new acquaintances. He was able to hold his own in their verbal exchanges, and they seemed warmly amused by his tenacity and hunger to learn. Paul had an uncanny ability to absorb and assimilate language. In no time, he had developed an adequate working knowledge of Russian. It was his fifth language.

Mutual camaraderie kept the hours and days passing in tolerable measures. Days passed; many more were ahead. It would take nearly five weeks to travel from one end of the massive continent to the other. Paul lost count after a while. Daylight and darkness bled one into the other as if there were no end to the cycle. When he was not immersed in conversation or sleep,

Paul stared quietly out the window at the passing landscape. It was stunning. The powerful steam engine pulled the freight over tall mountain peaks, showing the grandeur of Russia's expansive natural beauty.

The train stopped at stations at least once or twice a day. At each depot, hot food was brought in the cars and distributed to the soldiers. Paul was treated no differently than anyone else in the circulation of meals. He got out of his seat and took his place in the food line. And so it continued, for days and weeks. When the soldiers were fed, he was fed. While they traveled, they ate bread, kasha made from barley, and occasionally sausage. What little food they had, they shared. Some of the soldiers offered Paul cigarettes, but he respectfully declined the kindness, not offering an explanation. He was grateful for the affable nature of these Russian men and worried about their fate at the end of the line. It was never spoken, but in lengthy periods of silence, an uneasy sadness hung in the air. Many of his new friends would never return home to their families.

After nearly a month, they came to the end station in Vladivostok. Paul had not ceased to inquire about Lucy every place they had stopped. Indeed, many young Jewish women and orphaned girls had found refuge in Russia, but no one had heard of Lucy Argiewicz. Now Paul stood on the Kamchatka Peninsula — the end of the line, the end of the world — with nowhere else to look. He had searched three countries, traveled through ten time zones, covered mountain ranges and countless cities. He had exhausted all known possibilities and could not imagine what to do or where to go from here. He considered the option of continuing on to Manchuria or China with the Russians, but to what end? Certainly, his sister would not have traveled so far. For the first time since his search began, Paul was tempted to give up. He walked aimlessly around Vladivostok without food, shelter, or money for provisions.

The city was surrounded by electrified fences. Contrary to his experience, however, these fences were not raised to keep *people* in, but rather to keep *bears* out. Before the electric barriers were installed, residents were killed and eaten by the intruders. Dead grizzlies lined the ground on the opposite side. Paul observed from a safe distance; he had never seen such enormous

88

animals. He shook his head at the absurdity: How ironic, he thought, to be thankful to be *inside* of a fence.

The vast majority of people on the peninsula were Asian, so when Paul's eyes locked with those of another Caucasian, the two men were drawn together.

"Hello," the man spoke in German, extending a warm handshake.

"Hi! How ya doin'? You're German?" Paul replied in German but with the nuances of an American GI. He returned a firm but friendly grip accompanied by an inquisitive expression. His delight in meeting another European radiated from a broad smile.

"Yes, I am! And you? You speak with a Bavarian accent. Are *you* German?" He handed Paul a small piece of bread that he had obviously been saving. "I'm sorry, I don't have money to buy you a hot meal, but please take this. We can always find bread and coffee here. What I have is yours. Come, let's talk!"

Paul accepted the bread with gratitude and introduced himself as they walked together down the road. He explained how he had come to have a Bavarian German accent, but that he was also fluent in Polish, Yiddish, Czech, and well on his way to mastering Russian. He knew some words in French, English, and Hebrew, too, but did not consider his skill level in those languages to be anywhere near worth bragging about yet.

"So you're Jewish?"

"Yes."

"And you're *how* old?"

"I'll be sixteen soon."

The man fell silent for a few moments. "Sixteen. It sounds to me like you have a story to tell, my young friend. I'd like to hear about your life, Paul. How is it that you have ended up here at the end of the world at such a young age?"

They found a bench in the city and sat together for hours. As Paul began to relate his story, he felt as though an internal seal had burst, releasing an endless torrent of thoughts and memories. He told the man everything. He could barely breathe as he spoke of his family and the mounting fear that they had perished at the hands of evil men. The initial expression

89

of curiosity on the man's face faded, giving way to a weighted, grave visage. His dark brow furrowed between his eyes and he listened intently while Paul chronicled his life.

In the recounting of his story, a visible, festering anger began to emerge. Brief interludes of quiet were followed by eruptions of tears, fury, and vows of revenge. Paul pulled his concealed knife from his boot.

"If *anyone* comes near me again, I swear, I'll . . . " he thrust the knife into the open space before him as though piercing a would-be assailant.

The stranger opened his mouth to speak but hesitated and then pressed his lips together. He was a much older man whose demeanor revealed something beyond sympathy; it was more akin to empathy. His aging eyes bore no judgment, no condemnation, no rebuke — merely kindness and compassion, mercy and tenderness. He appeared to embody the kind of wisdom that one inherits only through suffering, yet he interjected neither opinion nor counsel. Instead, he granted Paul his absolute attention as the youth elaborated on the brutalities of the camps. The man's eyes followed imaginary lines in the dirt beneath his feet. Somehow, it seemed more reverent than staring at the young narrator's face. Finally, Paul stopped speaking, and almost indiscernibly the stranger nodded his head.

They spent the next several days together, living on the streets of Vladivostok, surviving on bread and the occasional offerings of locals. The man had little, but everything he had, he shared with Paul. He had been reading a Bible when they first met. Its black leather cover was worn and creased, its pages crumbled on the edges from having been handled so frequently. He carried it with him as though it bore in those tattered pages the very substance of life. He was a Jehovah's Witness missionary, which, despite his pure German ancestry, made him an enemy of the state. He, like Paul, was nothing more than a number to the Nazis — a despicable excuse for a human being, with no value or purpose. He had been liberated from Dachau, where he had spent five years as a political prisoner. He had been tortured and nearly killed more times than he could remember. Still, he had not abandoned his faith, as so many others had. He had often been asked by fellow prisoners how he could continue believing in a God who would allow such horrors to occur in the world. No one could be expected to answer such

90

a question, yet for him, there was nothing else. His devotion to his faith was the driving force of his life.

"Paul," he spoke gently to his young friend, "I have heard your story and I understand your pain. I know how much you miss your family and I feel the anger in your heart. Everything you love has been stolen from you and terrible things have happened . . . *terrible* things. No one should ever see or experience the horrors that you and I have. But we are powerless to change what has happened to us, to the people we love, or to the millions who have died. You are a good person, and you have the potential to be a great man — a man who can make a difference in the world. But right now, your mind is set on evil, and your soul is living in a dark and dangerous place. If you remain there, your life will be wasted. Nothing good can come from the type of revenge you seek. I am not going to try to convert you to Christianity, Paul, but I *am* going to convert you back to humanity. I want you to throw that knife away. That is *not* a knife for slicing bread. It is an evil *weapon* with only one purpose — to kill another human being. Throw it away."

Paul resisted the missionary's challenge. "You don't understand."

"Yes, I *do* understand, but this is not the right path. Throw the knife away." In his voice was a familiar authority, stern in its resolve, yet reflecting the depth of concern that a father feels for a beloved son. He remembered his own father's strict rebuke when he caught his son smoking filthy cigarette butts from the city streets. Paul continued to defend his right to exact his revenge for a while, but soon gave in to the voice of reason, the voice of wisdom.

The two walked to a municipal garbage basket on the street.

"Throw it in."

Paul hesitated. "I can't. You do it. Here." He extended the knife.

He shook his head. "No, I'm not going to touch that thing. *You* throw it away. Do it now." Paul wrapped the knife in a piece of discarded newspaper and buried it under several layers of trash. He stepped back from the receptacle and looked to the missionary for approval. The man smiled and put his arm around the back of Paul's shoulders as they walked away. "I'm proud of you," he said.

It was all Paul needed to hear.

"I want you to go back home, Paul. You don't belong here. You should be with your own people. Marry a nice Jewish girl, and raise Jewish children. If your parents have indeed perished, this is how you can honor their memory, God rest their souls. You're young and strong and have your whole life ahead of you. Go back to Europe and live your life as a Jew. Don't ever let anyone make you feel ashamed of who you are."

The air bore the chill of the changing season. If Paul were to leave Asia, he would have to do so immediately, before the cold descended. He had seen the enormous snow plows in the city; they were capable of moving drifts twenty feet high. He boarded the train the following week, waved to the man whom he would forever remember as "the one who converted him back to humanity," and headed west on the Trans-Siberian Railway.

The Russian soldiers he traveled with were battle-worn and weary. Still, they were generous and friendly. And they seemed to enjoy talking with the spunky teenager. Some of the young men were barely his age, and they spent hours exchanging stories of battles, camps, and death. He continued to ask about Lucy in every town and station where they stopped, even though he had surrendered the hope of finding her.

They pulled into a town in the Ukraine, not far from Kiev. Paul got off the train and stretched his legs in the station. He exited the building and walked down the road into the town. As was his habit, he inquired of the townspeople about any Jewish girls who might have recently arrived in the area. The Ukraine had a reputation for being especially anti-Semitic and many thousands of Jews had been killed there, so prudence demanded that he use caution. There were, indeed, many young Jewish people who had fled to the surrounding areas, but as always, none of the leads led him to Lucy. Frustrated, Paul returned to the station.

A couple of Orthodox Jewish youths sat on a bench by the tracks. He struck up a friendly conversation, speaking to the boys in the language of their fathers.

"Atah Y'hudi?" they asked. "Ken, ani Y'hudi,"[49] he responded with a smile.

---

[49] "Are you Jewish?" "Yes, I am Jewish."

They wore *tzitzit*,[50] *kipahs*,[51] and the traditional *payot*,[52] which left no question about their ethnic identity. Paul's family did not keep the same customs in their home, so the boys were surprised to hear him speak in their native tongue. They were gaunt, had dark circles under their eyes, and looked weak. He wondered if they, too, had been victims of Nazi cruelties or if they were just very poor and did not have money for food. This was a common occurrence, as discrimination against Russian Jews prevented them from receiving regular pay for their work. Many lived on only a few dollars a month, when there was money at all. While they spoke, a pair of stocky Ukrainian boys appeared from behind and began to harass them.

"We want to hear you say *kukuruza*."[53] The Jewish boys remained silent, knowing they were being taunted and that pronouncing the word with their Jewish accents was a setup.

"Say it, Jew!" they threatened.

Because Paul had learned the language directly from Russians, he did not have an incriminating Jewish accent. He knew what they were up to.

"What do you want? What business is it of yours?" Paul placed himself between his friends and the bullies. "Get out of here!"

"You get out of *our* way! This doesn't concern you," they retorted and began to push him. Paul had recovered a good deal of his strength and was vastly more muscular than either of the Ukrainians. If he had kept his knife, he would have used it. He had been witness to murder, torture, and beatings daily in the camps. It would mean nothing to him to kill these boys. Unleashed fury took over and he became like a wild beast, striking one of the bullies in the throat. The boy fell backward onto the track.

---

[50] *Tzitzit* (Hebrew, pro. TZEE-TZEET) knotted fringes on the corners of garments to remind the children of Israel to keep the commandments of the Torah.

[51] *Kipah* (Hebrew, pro. KEE pah) also known as a yarmulke in Yiddish; a head covering worn by observant Jews.

[52] *Payot* (Hebrew, pro. pay OHT or Yid. PAY os) Based on a command from the Torah that the Children of Israel abstain from cutting the hair from the "corners of their heads," the payot are the uncut portion of hair of the temples and sideburns, often appearing in locks, and sometimes tucked behind the ear.

[53] *Kukuruza* (Russian, pro. koo-koo-ROO-tzuh) corn. The Russian Jews had a slight (but telling) difference in the pronunciation of the word.

93

"If you're looking for trouble, you're going to get it!" he screamed at the other. "Now get out of here!" The boy turned and ran, leaving his companion behind.

"Disappear!" Paul yelled at his new friends. "Disappear!" The Jewish youths ran out of sight just as a train pulled into the station. It slowed but did not stop, and Paul grabbed hold of the rail, pulling himself into the car. He found a seat and settled in with a new batch of Russian soldiers. In a short while, he was able to regain his composure and put the incident behind him.

It was time to make a plan. Where would he go from here? He had been gone for months and still had no word of Lucy or anyone else in his family. He contemplated his options and decided that it was time to return to Bielsko. Perhaps by some miracle, they too had survived. Where would they go if not home? He had not been to Aleksandrowice since the day he and his father left. He leaned toward the window and looked ahead of the train at a glowing amber sunset.

For the first time in a span of seemingly infinite days, he allowed himself to think of home. He recalled the looks and smells of his house — burning coal in the ceramic furnace, his mother's cooking, their vegetable garden, the secret places in the woods where Noah had taken him on father-son walks. He indulged the memories and hoped with the innocence of youth. But in his mind, the persistent battle raged. He had learned better than to invest energy in optimism. Such luxuries were reserved for childhood, and those years were entombed in the camps. In place of the hope he craved, there simmered a hardness that demanded something else, something dark.

Home

To the horror of the Polish people, their beloved motherland had once again been overrun, their autonomy dismantled. The already destabilized country had buckled under the devastation of the war, and the defeat of Germany made Poland a relatively easy conquest. Treaties cemented the deal and Russia moved back in. Poles lashed out in frustration, relying on the usual prejudices to satiate their anger. Those who were inclined to irrational racial hatred resorted yet again to a blatant, unabashed anti-Semitism.

94

As he traveled through the country, Paul quickly learned to avoid German and Polish vigilantes who continued to murder Jewish people in the streets. Armed Russian soldiers patrolled the cities but often turned a blind eye, allowing the violence to persist. Some of the Russians even participated in ongoing pogroms against Jews who had returned from the camps — Jews who had survived years of Nazi atrocities only to die at the hands of their own neighbors and countrymen.

Paul traveled the back roads of the mountains. It took several days to reach Bielsko. He was weary and aching, but he was almost home. After five devastating years of being torn from his family, he could barely restrain the burning anticipation of seeing them again. His body and mind were filled with what felt like electrical charges shooting currents of power to his legs. His pace involuntarily quickened as he ran to Aleksandrowice, sprinting down the familiar gravel road that led to their house. As he approached it, he slowed to a stop and watched from a distance. Strangers tended the garden in his yard and walked confidently into and out of *his* house. They had stolen his home. His family was not there.

He hesitated for a few moments, not quite sure of his next move. He chose a familiar path. He walked through the town to the schoolhouse, keeping his face low as he went. People seemed defensive and hostile as he moved down the road. They stared at him as though his sole purpose for coming to their town was to commit some horrific act. He did not recognize anyone, and he looked no one in the eye. He didn't know if they were Polish, Russian, or German, and at this point, it didn't really matter. He just wanted to find his family.

He continued toward the school, his mind flooding with his memories of the familiar route. Livestock still roamed the streets — it was nice that something had remained unchanged. He hoped his principal would be at home. He and his wife had lived in the schoolhouse for as long as Paul could remember.[54] They had always been very kind, generous people. The fact that they were devout Catholics and he was Jewish had never been an issue. In fact, he rather enjoyed learning their prayers and customs, especially those

---

[54] The Polish government provided housing quarters for principals and their families inside the school buildings.

95

related to Christmas and Easter since it was on those days that children were showered with presents and magnificent things to eat. He remembered how loving and warm they had been to him.

"Please, God, let them be home. Please, God, hear my prayer."

He repeated the words incessantly until he reached the school. He knocked at the door, making his supplication one last time. He waited. He knocked again. Finally, the sound of footsteps became audible, and to his delight, the principal's wife opened the door.

"Hello. I am Paul Argiewicz. Do you remember me?"

"Yesus, Maria!" She dropped what was in her hand, grabbed Paul, and pulled him firmly against her. She held him in a powerful embrace, stroking his hair, kissing his face, and sobbing with unbridled emotion. Her body shook. Her tears mingled with his as she pressed his smooth face against her wrinkled cheek. Paul returned the embrace and struggled to contain his own emotion. Between sobs, she cried, "Yesus, Maria, thank you! Oh, God, thank you!" She cried the words over and over. She wept for several minutes, the whole while keeping her desperate grip on the boy. Paul didn't mind — it felt good to be so loved. Though he fought to maintain control of his emotions, his restraint shattered and he dissolved in a rush of tears. She held him in her arms as a mother would hold a wounded child, beckoning the release of the excruciating pain that bound him. His head cradled against her cheek; his tears soaked her shoulder.

"Do you know where my family is?" Somehow he managed to get the words out of his trembling body.

She hesitated, released her hold, and stepped back from him. She looked away and shook her head. "They were taken to Auschwitz, Paul. I don't think they survived." Paul closed his eyes, battling the disturbing images of his parents and sisters in that place. Flashes of brutality darted through his brain. Shootings, beatings, stabbings, torture — it was too much to bear in the moment. He struggled hard to dismiss the pictures from his mind. There was nothing definite, nothing official — not yet. As long as there remained reason to hope, Paul would not stop looking for them.

"Come with me." The woman took his hand and led him to a small wooden table. Poised in the center was a tall glass jar containing a white pillar

96

candle. The flame flickered only slightly when it was touched by the breeze from their movement.

"You see this, Paul? I lit a candle for you the day you disappeared. I have kept a light burning all these years. This has been here every day, shining for heaven to see, a light for God to remember and protect you. Not a day has passed since you left that I have not prayed for your safety and your return home. Until today, there has been no news of you. Now, I see God has answered my prayers." She raised her fingers to his face and swept his dark hair back from his forehead. She stroked his wet cheek, wiped away a tear, and then bent over the table. She paused for an instant and then blew out the candle. He watched as the extinguished flame gave way to a thin stream of white smoke. The stream widened and swirled at the top, engulfing a small crucifix that hung above it on the wall.

"What should I do? I have to find them. Where should I look?" His eyes pleaded but did not depart from the rising smoke. Though she believed his family to be dead, she said nothing more about it.

"Paul, you have to leave. You cannot stay here. It's too dangerous. These people . . . they will kill you. Get out of Poland as soon as you can. Go through the mountains to Czechoslovakia. You will be safer there."

The principal's wife took him outside to a shed behind the school and gave him her husband's bicycle.[55] She pointed him in the direction of the Czech border. "That is where you want to go. Whatever you do, stay away from the cities," she told him. "Go straight across the border and don't look back. Wait here for just a minute." She ran back into the house. Paul looked at the distant mountains. Nothing seemed very far anymore. The world somehow felt a much smaller place since the last time he stood on this soil. He reviewed the directions she had given him and plotted his route. It should not take that long on a bicycle, he thought. The woman hurried back to him with a loaf of bread and a manageable quantity of food for his trip. She wrapped it in a large cloth and secured it to the rear of the bike. She hugged him one last time. "Go in safety, Paul. I will be praying for you. Just remember what I told you."

---

[55] The principal of the school had died the previous year.

97

Back in Hof

After having traveled on foot for so many days to reach his home, Paul left Aleksandrowice within a few short hours. He rode the old, rusty bicycle through the mountains and hills, across deep valleys, and through Czech villages. He took the widow's advice and avoided major cities, all the while mindful to be as inconspicuous as possible. A little more than a week later, he returned to Hof and to his American friends. The chaplain offered a prayer of thanksgiving for his safe return and helped him find an apartment in town.

Paul went back to UNRRA to reclaim his job. They rehired him immediately. The organization needed the extra help, particularly where the displaced Jewish population was concerned. It was a monumental task providing help to thousands of starving, sick, and homeless people. Employing a Jewish worker who spoke Yiddish, Czech, German, Polish, and Russian was a novelty. Not only was he able to speak to the people in their native tongue, but because of his own experience in the concentration camps, he was uniquely qualified to recognize, appreciate, and address their specific needs.

He drove the same two-ton military trucks that he had driven previously and delivered supplies to the transitional camps. However, the influx of people into Hof had slowed considerably, as the ruling authorities of the East Zone had clamped down on the mass exodus of refugees from those countries. Just as Ziemack had foretold months earlier, they were no longer able to get out of the Russian-occupied territories. One of Paul's assignments involved driving to the border, smuggling people out of Czechoslovakia, and transporting them to a transitional camp in Germany. The Rosenthal China Company had a large factory between Hof and the East Zone border that had been converted to a place of temporary lodging. It was filled with rows of cots and supplies. There, hundreds of refugees were dropped off, cared for by the American forces, and lodged until they could be picked up by the next available truck.

For months, the process of shuttling and relaying crowds of people from the border to the factory and from the factory to Hof continued without major incident. Once in Hof, they stayed either in the converted tavern or in the larger camp that had been built from old German army barracks. There, they were able to rethink their lives and formulate a plan for their future. Those who were fortunate enough to locate surviving family members moved to wherever they had settled. That, however, was not the norm. The more common scenario saw people alone and on their own in the world. They were battered, shaken, and altered, but they were alive. Some took jobs locally and settled permanently in Germany. Others moved out of Europe altogether and relocated to the United States or South America, or later made *aliyah*[56] to the newly birthed state of Israel. Whatever their destiny, the American soldiers saw to it that many thousands of Jewish people were given a new chance at life.

Between delivering food and transporting people from one area to another, Paul was given additional assignments. He ran various "secret errands" for the organization. Wherever they told him to go, he went, and whatever they told him to do, he did. Once or twice a week, he smuggled crated guns and ammunition that had been confiscated from the Czech Communists. Under "silent orders" from government officials, he drove the crates to Jewish transition camps outside of Munich. From there, the weapons were transported out of the country. He was not supposed to know what was concealed in the crates, but there was very little that got by Paul. He was observant, smart, and suspicious. He was a survivor.

Working for UNRRA had its fringe benefits. Because American combat troops had been demobilized in Germany and replaced by occupying forces, loads of combat military supplies were discarded or left behind. Paul purchased a Harley Davidson motorcycle for $10. It had a *Military Police* decal on the windshield, which he was instructed to remove, although it was tempting to leave such an intimidating memento in place. He drove the vehicle all around Germany, and by the end of two years, he was familiar with most of the country. There were very few places, save the East Zone, that remained uncharted territory.

Paul's job supplied him with frequent adventures. On one assignment, he traveled by train to Munich to obtain requisition papers for refugees to

---

[56] *Aliyah* (Hebrew, pro. ah-lee-YAH or ah-LEE-yah) literally "to go up" or "ascend"; used in reference to the obtaining of citizenship in Israel.

99

leave the country. All the sleeping compartments were occupied by American GIs. The soldiers locked the doors to the rooms and sprawled out over the entire area, leaving no space for anyone else to sit.

Paul approached one of the locked compartments and knocked on the door. "May I sit down, please?" Two of the soldiers ignored the request as if he had not even spoken. Another turned his head over his shoulder and made a snide remark. They were not about to budge, nor was Paul about to stand on his feet for the entire trip. He was annoyed by their rudeness. He waited for the GI to turn his head away and then slipped a limburger cheese[57] sandwich under the seat, next to a radiator. He waited in the hallway outside, amused by his ingenuity. Within a few minutes, the sleeping compartment was filled with a pungent, horrible smell and the young men rushed out of the room.

"What the hell did you do?" one of the GIs shouted at the others.

"*I* didn't do anything! Let's get outta here, man!"

Paul smiled, recovered his now-warm cheese sandwich, and stretched out on one of the beds in the sleeping compartment.

● ● ●

Paul returned to Hof and resumed his regular duties. On a routine delivery in the camp one afternoon, he jumped out of the truck and walked around to the back to unload boxes. As he carried the food to the door of the barracks, he heard a vaguely familiar voice from behind.

"Hey, Argiewicz!"

Paul turned and was amazed to see his old friend Bob standing across the street.

"Oy vey!" Paul looked to heaven and laughed. "I don't believe it!" Paul set the box on the ground and ran to Bob. The small-town buddies threw their arms around each other and embraced enthusiastically.

"You've grown up, Paul!" Paul was an eleven-year-old child the last time Bob saw him. Now the little kid from his hometown towered over him.

"Yeah, I suppose I have," Paul replied. They scheduled a time to meet that evening to catch up on each other's lives. Paul finished his day's work

---

[57] Limburger is a soft white cheese that has an extraordinarily pungent odor and taste.

100

and hurried to meet his friend. They talked for hours about their families, the war, their experiences, and the future. They agreed there was no going back to Poland. There were no Jewish communities remaining there; there was nothing to hold them together. The synagogues had been burned, the cemeteries desecrated, and the Jews who remained were forced to live in hiding. Anti-Semitism was still rampant.

Bob's *mishpucha*[58] was gone. He explained that his father had been captured years earlier and taken to a concentration camp in Russia. As far as Bob knew, he was either still imprisoned or, more likely, was dead. Bob had been left to care for his mother and grandmother in Bielsko. When the family was ordered to the train station to be transferred to the ghetto, Bob approached the train with his mother and grandmother. His ailing grandmother did not have the strength to step up onto the boxcar. "Get on the train, Jew!" the officer shouted in German. The old woman struggled but, despite desperate attempts, was unable to climb onto the stair. Without hesitation, the Nazi lifted the wooden butt of his rifle over his head and with alarming force, struck the frail woman repeatedly until she fell, bloodied and limp, to the ground. Bob's mother screamed and ran to aid her dying mother. Within a matter of seconds she, too, lay dead. The Nazis showed no mercy for the weakness of old age or the weakness of compassion. The blood of mother and daughter mingled on the hard pavement.

Bob spent nearly five years in the camps, and like Paul, had miraculously survived. His sister had not — she had been murdered in Auschwitz. Now he was one of the millions who found himself alone. Bob was making plans to move to America.

Paul was thrilled to have his old friend in his life again. They saw each other regularly after their reunion. They found comfort in the familiarity of each other's company, their talks about home, and their precious shared memories. Even the company of his closest friend, however, could not soothe the ache in Paul's life. He still clung to the hope that he might find someone — anyone — in his family.

● ● ●

---

[58] *Mishpucha* (Hebrew/Yiddish, pro. mihsh-PUHK-uh) family.

101

It was a routine mission — nothing out of the ordinary. Paul was on the Autobahn, driving a U.S. military transport truck to Munich. Two teenage girls were hitchhiking on the side of the road. They each carried a bag tied to a stick over their shoulder. One of the girls wore a striped concentration camp uniform. Paul pulled the truck over and offered them a lift. They climbed in the front seat, smiled, and thanked him in Czech. Because he wore an UNRRA uniform and drove a U.S. Army vehicle, they presumed him to be an American GI. They conversed quietly among themselves, assuming he did not understand. One of the girls was from Czechoslovakia and the other from Poland. They were both Jewish.

"Are you hungry?" Paul spoke to the girls in Yiddish. They looked at each other in amazement. He smiled and explained that he, too, was Jewish and that he had been liberated from Buchenwald. The girls began to cry and told him that they had not eaten in over two days. Paul turned off the highway and into a remote area. Taking them to the back of the fully loaded truck, he opened cans of food and collected fresh water from a crevice in a mountain rock. He stood by them and watched as the starving girls sat on the ground and ate their first decent meal in weeks.

"I've been looking for my sister. Have you ever heard of a girl named Lucy Argiewicz?" Paul asked in Yiddish, preparing himself for disappointment even before finishing his question. One of the girls stopped eating and stood up. She looked at him for a moment in silence as she finished swallowing a mouthful of food and then walked to the truck. She retrieved the bag with her belongings and untied it from the stick. Standing next to him, she handed him a group photograph that had been taken of young female survivors from Auschwitz.

"Can you find her in this picture?" Her eyes moved from the photo to his face then back to the photo. "Is she in the picture?"

Paul was silent, his eyes fixated on a single face on the paper. His hands began to shake as he pointed to it.

"This is my sister. This is Lucy." He spoke the words quietly at first and then repeated them louder as tears spilled over his cheeks. He could feel the blood coursing through his veins. "This is her! This is my Lucy!" Paul

102

clutched the photograph. "She's alive! Oh, thank you, God!" His eyes turned back to the girl. "Where is she? Where is my sister?"

"Lucy is a friend of mine." The girl's voice quivered as she spoke. "I've just come from her. She is in the East Zone in Czechoslovakia, about 160 kilometers from here."[59]

Paul determined Lucy's exact location, drove the girls to their destination, and completed his business in Munich. As he sped back to Hof, he devised a plan to smuggle Lucy out of Czechoslovakia. It would be difficult and dangerous, but nothing would stop him from claiming his sister.

● ● ●

It would be impossible for Paul to accomplish his mission legally. He would have to convince someone in the U.S. Army to forge a requisition for a military jeep, as such rescues and reclamations were simply not sanctioned by the armed forces. Furthermore, the borders between the East and West were tightly guarded. Armed Russian and Czech patrols were posted on every major road on the east side of the line. American, British, French, and German police took their posts on the west. All vehicles, especially military vehicles, crossing from one zone to the other were subject to inspection or interrogation at the checkpoints. The main highways, particularly on the Czech side, were not an option. Paul would have to figure out an alternate route.

The only people who were exempt from inspections on either side of the border were local farmers. They were given permission to travel on special roads that were short distances from the highway. Inspection of daily loads of grain and other crops proved too costly, time-consuming, and inefficient, so farmers moved without restraint from Czechoslovakia into and out of Germany without the nuisance of patrol interference. The farming villages on the border also had large open spaces where cattle roamed freely and farmers worked the fields. Since the villages were not subject to the scrutiny of the authorities, Paul would travel these areas whenever they were accessible. He hoped that would reduce the risk of being caught.

A sympathetic Jewish friend at the U.S. Army base in Hof forged and signed a requisition for a jeep. Because it was not a certified form, he rubbed the imprint of a coin on the paper to make it appear official. He also handed

---

[59] 160 kilometers is approximately equal to 100 miles.

103

Paul a loaded .45 automatic pistol with an extra clip, should he "run into any trouble." If either of the men were caught at any point in the venture, the soldier would be subject to military disciplinary action, perhaps even resulting in a dishonorable discharge from the service. It was a significant risk, but one he felt justified in taking. In his thinking, how could he not help in this very small way to right one of the millions of wrongs in this war? If he could be instrumental in reuniting even one family, he would be content that he had done something worthwhile.

Paul had his jeep. He filled the tank with gasoline and loaded two extra five-gallon gas cans on the back for the return trip. Every move would have to be meticulously calculated and executed with absolute precision. There was no room for error. He placed the gun on the seat next to him and took off from the base, heading east on a main thoroughfare out of Germany. Paul wore his official UNRRA uniform and hat — it gave him the appearance of an American GI.

As he approached the border checkpoint, he held his "requisition form" tightly in his hand. He flashed the paper and a friendly smile at the GI patrol, ensuring that the imprint of the coin was visible. The GI nodded and saluted Paul. One down. He held his breath as he drove across the border into the East Zone. No one on the Czech side even bothered to stop him — he may as well have been invisible, he thought. He laughed nervously for just a second, inhaled a deep breath, and continued on his way until he reached the small village where Lucy lived. When he arrived at the house, a young woman was hanging wet laundry on the clothesline in the yard. He pulled up next to the house and smiled at her. She looked over her shoulder at the Yankee jeep and then at Paul.

"May I help you?" she asked, looking somewhat concerned.

"I hope so," he answered in Czech. "I am looking for Lucy Argiewicz. Is she home?"

The girl stopped her chore and turned to face him. "Why do you want to see Lucy?"

"Just get her, please."

"One minute." She walked to the house and yelled to the basement.

"Lucy! There is an American soldier here to see you! Come quickly!"

104

Paul's heart raced in his chest and his mouth grew so dry that he was unable to swallow. His breathing quickened, making him lightheaded. Was this really happening? He tapped his fingers against his legs to make sure he wasn't dreaming. Within a minute, Lucy emerged from the house.

"Yes? May I help you?" she spoke in Czech. Paul hesitated for a moment, restraining the surge of emotion.

"Hello, Lucy." She did not recognize him. The last time she saw Paul, he was a little boy in rags. Now he was a grown man in an American military uniform.

"I have good news for you." He struggled to remain composed. "I am here to let you know that your brother is alive. I've just come from him in Bavaria. He wants you to know that he is well and safe."

"My brother? Paul?" She began to cry. "Where is he? Why didn't he come to tell me himself?"

Paul could not restrain himself any longer. He reached for his sister. "I am your brother, Lucy. I am Paul."

He pulled her to him and held her, stroking her soft, dark hair as they wept.

"Mama . . . Papa . . . Phella," she cried.

"I know, Lucy. I know. It'll be okay. I'm going to take care of you now." He continued holding and rocking her for a few more minutes. "Get your things, sweetheart. We have to leave now."

Lucy ran into the house to gather her possessions. She came out with pots, pans, and an armful of junk.

"No, no. We don't have time for that! We have ten minutes, Lucy. We've got to get out of here *now!* Just get what you absolutely need." Paul was growing anxious. If they drew too much attention in the village or were caught trying to escape from the East Zone, they would be arrested and thrown into a Communist prison. They would be separated forever. The sooner they got out, the better.

He hurried to get his sister and her few essentials into the jeep and drove toward the farming villages west of them. The dirt road they were on led to a large open field near the border. Herds of cattle and random vegetation were framed by trees in the distance. The West Zone was just on the

105

other side. Paul looked around, and over each shoulder. There was no one in sight, not even farmers working their fields. He depressed the accelerator pedal as far as he could without sending the jeep out of control. Lucy was mildly annoyed.

"Why are you driving so fast? Stop driving so fast!"

He pulled into a ravine behind some bushes and stopped the jeep. "Get down," he instructed her. Paul looked to the patrol booth less than half a kilometer away. He took the gun from under the seat and positioned it in his hand. He would not hesitate to use it if circumstances made it necessary. There were two Czech guards and two Russian guards on the east side of the border. They were engaged in conversation, making plans to have a little party on the job. Because there were no cars coming through, they left the booth unattended and went off to drink some vodka. Paul couldn't believe his eyes.

"How can this be? They can't do that!" he chuckled to himself.

"How can *what* be? Who can't do *what?*" Lucy was crouched below the window.

"Shh. It's okay. Never mind. We're almost home, Lucy. It's a miracle! Just one more . . . one more."

He threw the jeep into four-wheel drive and floored it across the border. There were American and German police at the west side checkpoint. The jeep kicked up the dirt on the road, leaving a cloud of dust behind them. The guards at the booth noticed, but Paul did not slow down. He kept driving as though he were entitled to be on that road. There was a space in the barbed wire fencing about the width of a driveway. He headed straight for it. Because of the markings on the jeep, the border police assumed that he was an American GI. They waved to him. Paul waved back. He laughed and pulled Lucy's head to his lips. He kissed her hair and laughed again, shaking his head. "It's a miracle," he told her. "It's a miracle!"

They had crossed the border.

Paul dropped Lucy at his apartment in Hof and hurried to return the jeep before anyone discovered it was missing. His ally was waiting anxiously.

"Did you find her? Is she here? Did you use the gun?" Paul's accomplice fired a string of questions faster than Paul could answer.

"Everything is fine, *Baruch HaShem!* Lucy is here safely and I didn't have to use the gun, thank God." Paul's eyes welled with tears. "I traveled over 12,000 miles — through ten time zones — to find my sister and the whole time she was only a few hours away." He hugged the American soldier and thanked him for his help. "God will reward you. You have done a great *mitzvah,* my friend."

When Paul returned to his apartment, Lucy had converted the tiny one-room space into two rooms by hanging a sheet from the ceiling. He smiled pensively as he recalled how his mother had done the same in their bedroom at home. How alike they were, Lucy and Elka.

A New Home

Over the next several months, Paul continued his work with UNRRA, helping to rescue and rehabilitate Jewish refugees. Lucy also took a job with the organization, stamping permits for people to leave the country. Paul's old friend, Bob, frequently came to visit them at the apartment and in a short while, he and Lucy fell in love. He asked Paul for permission to marry his sister. Paul was delighted with the match, and Bob and Lucy were married by a rabbi in Hof a few months later. He gave the newlyweds the apartment and moved out to live on his own, though he spent much of his spare time with them.

Not long after getting married, Lucy received news that a friend from Czechoslovakia was coming to visit her in Hof. She was thrilled. The two girls had become companions in a work camp, where they had labored together sewing Nazi military uniforms. During their incarceration, the girl had often spoken about her brother whom she had not seen in years. She explained how the children in her family had been taken from their home, separated, and imprisoned. Although she had received no word of her brother since that day, she was hoping now to find him in Germany. She comforted herself with the thought that he might be found among the survivors.

Through his contacts at UNRRA, Paul was able to use the little information he had to locate Lucy's friend's long-lost brother. After picking him up near the Czech border, Paul brought him to the apartment, where Lucy's friend waited anxiously. The emotional reunion of brother and sister filled

107

Paul with a sense of thankfulness as he considered his own good fortune. What a miracle, he thought, to have his own beloved sister Lucy at his side. Such a miracle . . . If only Phella . . . He stifled the thought — it was too painful.

That evening, the five survivors shared their stories. Each recounted horrors, tragedies, and miracles they had experienced in the various camps. For the first time, Lucy told Paul what life had been like after his arrest. Their father had returned to the ghetto that dark day devastated at the sight of Paul locked in the detainment center. Noah knew he might never see his son again. The family had never ceased to pray for his safety, and on August 6, Paul's 12th birthday, his father had wept bitterly. Lucy had been transported from the ghetto in Sosnowiec directly to a camp in Czechoslovakia, where she had worked as a seamstress during her imprisonment. All she knew about Noah, Elka, Phella, and Pinchas was that they had been taken to Auschwitz. She never saw them again. Telling her story, she paused for a moment and fixed her eyes on her young friend from Czechoslovakia. Their friendship had been such a well of comfort and hope in that place of horror. Lucy closed her eyes as a solitary tear ran down her cheek.

The girl's brother recounted a near-catastrophic experience in one of the camps. "We were working on a dam." His dark eyes moved sporadically as he visualized the memory. "The canal was at least a 30-foot drop. I was exhausted and starving. There were several armed Nazi guards keeping watch and they didn't let us rest . . . ever. We were all so weak, so tired. I lost my footing and fell into a powerful whirlpool in the river. I didn't have the strength to swim out of it and barely enough to hold my head out of the rushing water. I was starting to be pulled under by the whirlpool and would have promptly drowned. I remember the guards were holding their pistols and laughing, when suddenly a young man — another prisoner — jumped into the water. He swam to me and pulled me to safety! I didn't know what was happening. I thought the guards would shoot us both, but they didn't. We walked through the water to the bank and went back to work."

"I can't believe it!" Paul interrupted. "That was you?"

"What are you talking about?" The man was puzzled.

"That was me!" Paul told him excitedly. "I was the one who jumped in the river and saved you!" Paul shook his head and laughed as he told the story. "God works in such mysterious ways. I taught myself to swim at the age of five. The river near our home was one of our favorite play spots. My friends and I used to love to splash around in the water. I remember it was beautiful, clear mountain-fed water. Remember, Lucy?" His sister smiled and nodded as her younger brother reminisced about better times. "I was determined to swim, but the river had such a strong current and I didn't have the skill or the strength to stay afloat. So one day I marched into the local butcher shop and told the butcher, 'I need two big pig bladders — the biggest ones you have.' He was nice enough to give them to me. Can you imagine what he must have been thinking? I ran home and grabbed some string and took everything down to the river. I blew the bladders up like balloons, tied them together, and used my invention for a float. It worked great and that's how I learned to swim! I became a very strong swimmer that summer."

"That was you! Oy, my God! I recognize you now!" The man chuckled.

The two young men laughed and embraced and laughed some more.

"But how was it that you were able to jump in and save me? Why didn't the guards shoot you?"

"Let me tell you what happened," Paul continued. "When you fell into the canal, one of the guards drew his pistol to shoot you. The other guard stopped him and said, 'Save your bullet and let's watch him drown.' So, just as you were being caught in the whirlpool, I asked permission to jump in. They thought that was funny — two prisoners would drown together. It was great entertainment for them and they wouldn't have to waste their bullets." The room grew quiet and Paul hung his head. "Waste their bullets."

Paul had caught typhoid from the dirty river that day. A bacterial infection contracted through the ingestion of Salmonella-infested food or water, typhoid was common among prisoners in Nazi Germany. It caused a high fever, severe abdominal pain, and intestinal bleeding; it was often fatal. Paul became gravely ill and was taken to the "sick room" where diseased prisoners were quarantined and left to die. The Nazis kept their distance from the area to avoid exposure, and prisoners received no medical attention. Paul was surrounded by sick and dying men. He would have died himself had it

109

not been for the kindness of a German foreman who picked him up from the building every day and helped him walk to "work." The foreman gave him food and clean water, and allowed him to lie in the shade under a tree for the duration of the work day. When the SS guards threatened Paul, the man covered for him. The routine continued for a few weeks until Paul recovered. He never knew why the foreman showed him such kindness.

"So, you nearly died as a result of saving me?"

"But, just look at what happened." Paul grinned. "Another miracle! Another person who had the *rachmunus* to defy the evil. And here we are talking about it! That's the greatest miracle of all."

The evening was laced with bittersweet emotion and unanswered questions. Why should they have survived when so many perished? They all knew that answer would never come. Their lives would never return to what they once knew. They would be forever branded, numbered people. For whatever reason, they had lived. Ever-grieving testaments to the evil man can do, these were survivors of the Holocaust.

For those who had survived, the guilt of having lived was almost as terrible as the grief of having lost all those who had died or been killed. But, as these reluctant witnesses to history would discover daily with both pain and gratitude, life went on.

Bob and Lucy applied to the CIC[60] for a permit to immigrate to America. Due to the organization's thorough investigation of all applicants, the process took about a year to finalize. When they relocated to the United States the following year, Paul decided to follow. He, too, submitted an application to the CIC and began the rigorous process of questions, examinations, and research. He spent over 40 days in quarantine in Bremerhaven,[61] Germany, while the details of his future life were mapped out by strangers. Three criteria determined an applicant's acceptance into the United States. First, the applicant needed to be free of all communicable disease; second, the applicant had to be sponsored by an American agency and have a job established in the U.S.; and finally, the applicant could not be a burden on American taxpayers or

---

[60] The Counter Intelligence Corps, or CIC, was an American military intelligence organization predating the CIA.

[61] Bremerhaven is a German port city on the North Sea.

110

society. The requirements seemed more than reasonable and a small price to pay for what America offered her people.

Paul was sponsored by an American Jewish agency. It had lined up a place for him to live and secured a job where he would work as an electrician. When the five-week quarantine period was complete, he boarded the steamship *General Blackford* with approximately three thousand other passengers. He did not look back. For the next eight days, he would journey on the Atlantic Ocean, wrapped in the hope that America would indeed be the land of freedom, opportunity, and equality.

Food was limited and the men onboard received only two meals a day. Women and children were given preferential treatment, eating three times daily. Pregnant and nursing mothers and young children had exclusive rights to milk. The sea was turbulent, and most of the people onboard became extremely ill. Seasickness kept them from the mess hall when meals were served, so Paul — who was not at all affected by the ocean's choppiness — ate his fill.

It was night when they arrived at Ellis Island in New York City. The crew informed the passengers that it was Labor Day and the dockworkers were on holiday. No one understood exactly what that meant. Why would there be a holiday from labor? In any case, it meant they would have to wait until morning to disembark. The ship anchored in the harbor, and the weary passengers spent their last night on deck.

Paul sat on a small wooden folding chair overlooking the water and inhaled the air of the cool summer evening. It smelled different here. The salty ocean breeze blew his hair back from his forehead and he closed his eyes, granting himself permission to remember. He would not allow his thoughts to meander too far, though. The memories were too fresh, too painful. He tried to evoke pleasant images and recollections of his family, but flashes of their brutal end overpowered his will, and he had to force his eyes open to stop them. Noah, Elka, Phella, Pinchas, and most of his relatives had been murdered in the gas chambers of Auschwitz. Paul covered his eyes with the palms of his hands and shook his head in disbelief. "How can this be?" He submitted his request for an answer — he knew it was futile to ask.

111

It took hours for him to fall asleep that night. When he finally did drift off, sleep did not provide much-needed peace or rejuvenation. It never did anymore. Sleep had become a sadistic foe, an avenue through which all the horrors of his experience were granted unlimited access. He was no longer in the safe zone of consciousness where he could willfully manipulate the direction of his tormented mind. Rather, sleep launched him into the deepest recesses of the darkness — into nightmares of smoke, screams, executions, and skeletal bodies. It would not release him until he rose with the light of dawn.

In the semi-consciousness between sleep and waking, Paul heard orders being yelled. He woke in a sweat, not knowing where he was. Without opening his eyes, he listened. It did not sound like *kapos,* or police, or SS, thank God. It was the commotion of passengers organizing their belongings, and longshoremen[62] calling out as they unloaded the ship's cargo. He shook off the remnants of sleep and looked around. It took a few moments to adjust his thoughts. Oh yes, it was Tuesday morning . . . he was in America . . . he was safe. He was in America! Paul jumped from the edge of his bed and grabbed his few belongings. He sprinted onto the deck. A man he had befriended on the journey approached him with a message.

"Paul, there is a lady waiting to greet you."

"A lady? What lady?" Perhaps someone from the Jewish agency had boarded the ship to receive him. He smoothed his hair and clothing in preparation to meet her.

"No," the man said. "Come with me." He led him to the other side of the vessel. There in the harbor, towering above them, was the Statue of Liberty. Paul froze on the deck, entranced by the lady's beauty and power, paralyzed by her magnificence. His eyes widened as his gaze fixed on her form. Awe rendered him motionless and unable to speak. The man explained that she was America's most beloved symbol of freedom and then recited from memory the words engraved on the monument:

---

[62] dockworkers

112

Give me your tired, your poor,
Your huddled masses yearning to breathe free,
The wretched refuse of your teeming shore;
Send these, the homeless, tempest-tossed to me,
I lift my lamp beside the golden door.

Paul found it difficult to breathe. He was no longer in command of his body. His arms and legs trembled violently. His knees buckled under him. He fell onto the deck, sobbing intensely as the words on the monument reached out to him, to all those he carried in his heart who would never hear these words.

The man placed a sympathetic hand on his shoulder.

"Don't cry, Paul. Everything is going to be all right now, you'll see. You'll start a whole new life here."

Paul looked up at the lady in the harbor and stood to his feet. He inhaled a long, deep breath. "Tell me again what it says."

The man recited the inscription once more. He stood next to Paul for a few minutes, then turned and quietly walked away.

Paul's eyes never left the lady. He spoke in a whisper.

"I am tired and I am poor. I want to breathe free. I have stood in huddled masses and I have been branded as wretched refuse . . . a number. I am homeless and lost. If you will have me, I promise to do my best to bring you honor as long as I live in your land."

He looked at the statue for a little longer and then at the sky above her. He stood in quiet reverence, offering thanks and a blessing for the gift of life.

On September 6, 1949, Paul Argiewicz picked up his bag and walked off the ship into the waiting arms of his new home. ✡

113

Afterword

When meeting Paul for the first time, most people invariably come away with the impression that they have stumbled upon a true American patriot. And a patriot he is. Barely 19 years old when he arrived at Ellis Island in 1949, Paul wasted no time in studying for, and ultimately acquiring, his American citizenship. (His naturalization document may be seen in the photo section of this book.) It was one of the greatest days of his life.

Paul enlisted in the U.S. military a few years later where he faithfully served his country during the Korean War. After receiving an honorable discharge from the service, he settled in Sheboygan, Wisconsin, with a young wife and two sons. For years, he worked long, hard hours as an electrician. His skills in the trade and his ability to sustain a family by using them are a testament to the benevolence of Hans, Paul's former "boss" at Blechhammer.

Finally a world away from Nazi Germany, Paul was able to start his own business and earn his shot at the American dream. It was realized in Argo Heating and Refrigeration. After having gone for months without food only a few years earlier, Paul now had six freezers full. For all its blessings and sanctuary, he was grateful to his adopted country beyond measure. Having opened her arms to him, America received Paul's bravery, service, sacrifice, strength, and love in return.

And now a personal note (for this journey writing Paul's story has indeed been a labor of love and an honor on behalf of a man who has become a dear friend). My children insist that it is virtually impossible to be with Paul for more than a few minutes without acquiring a story to take home. "Things just happen when you're with Paul," my son says. He's right: Things just happen when you're with Paul. He is one of those rare and wonderfully unique people whose every hour contains a story. Any number of events drawn up from the well of his years could merit entire chapters of storytelling. For Paul has lived a storied life, and he is the quintessential storyteller — a fact that may easily be verified by 150-plus hours of recorded dialogue from days, weeks, and months spent around his kitchen table.

Paul is the only person I know who can strike up a conversation with a complete stranger at a Yukon Gold potato stand in northern Wisconsin, only to discover that the stranger had been a WWII soldier, and, as fate would have it, a Nazi concentration camp liberator. The two men would become lifelong friends. Likewise, I cannot recall ever having had the privilege of knowing a person who, due to the sheer integrity of his character and experience, could inspire a courtroom judge to descend from his bench and embrace him in the presence of dozens of witnesses. Is there another living soul who can be pulled over by a cop, convince the officer to buy him a cup of coffee for falsely accusing him of D.U.I., and end up talking (with the guy still on duty) for nearly two hours in a Burger King? Who else could charm a traffic court judge into reducing $1,500 worth of parking tickets down to 15 bucks? As I said, every day, every hour with Paul is a story.

He is a dying breed of man in our society, one who is as tough and immovable in his opinions and convictions as he is a pushover for small children. Father, grandpa, teacher, doctor, rabbi, veterinarian, cook, handyman, counselor — he can spontaneously assume whatever role might best deliver valuable insight. He can converse intelligently for hours on just about any subject, with just about anybody, in just about any language. He loves to laugh, to eat, to bargain shop, to play with his grandchildren and great grandchildren, but mostly, Paul Argiewicz loves to tell his stories. At almost 80 years of age, he is still sharp, grounded, masculine. And with his force of personality there is great wisdom — the kind that only seems to come with having survived insurmountable odds or unspeakable tragedy.

How then to capture a man like Paul, to accurately condense the events of his life, in a small book? These pages contain merely a glimpse — the skeleton and shadow — of the early life of this remarkable man. The true substance — the flesh and blood of his story — resides in the man himself.

If that substance must be summarized in parting words, let them be these: Paul Argiewicz has never met a stranger, cheated a helpless person, or taken advantage of another's fear, ignorance, or innocence for personal gain. Generosity toward his fellow man and a genuine concern for humanity are paramount in his worldview. He has not only endured and survived the incomprehensible nadir of human cruelty and depravity, but has overcome the most hideous of circumstances with grace, integrity, and forgiveness.

Time for one final story. In September of 2008, a small synagogue in the Chicago area hosted an unusual event. The guest speaker that Sabbath morning was Jobst Bittner, a German pastor from the town of Tubingen. Tubingen has long been considered one of the most notorious anti-Semitic strongholds in Germany. In the early 20th century, the town's university provided a safe haven for anti-Jewish thought, theology, and propaganda. And it gave rise to some of the most prominent leaders of the regime that would ultimately be responsible for the systematic murder of 12 million innocent people, half of whom were Jewish.

Pastor Bittner leads a church in Tubingen of about 300 evangelical Christians. Over two-thirds of the church's members are children or grandchildren of Nazis, many of whom were war criminals. These "children" have devoted their lives to the cause of repentance for the atrocities committed by their parents and their nation. They do not seek absolution, nor do they expect to be forgiven by the Jews of the world. Still, this congregation has consistently, tangibly, and lovingly reached out in service to the Jewish community and survivors of the Holocaust in ways that are as unique and innovative as they are radical and bold. They raise money, visit homes, and provide help and support through financial and human services. They march, preach, educate, assemble, peaceably demonstrate in town squares, host concerts and events, and effect change everywhere they go — and in everything they do.

Once a year, Pastor Bittner and his congregants travel on foot throughout Germany, preaching a message to their countrymen. The subject: the evil of anti-Semitism. Retracing the routes of the Death Marches — the very roads once stained with innocent blood during the Holocaust — these spiritual mavericks walk hundreds of miles on what they refer to as the March of Life. Deeply embedded in Pastor Bittner's message of repentance, however, are also words of hope, love, forgiveness, and reconciliation. To the broken and remorseful people of Germany — those who continue to grapple with the shame of their nation's guilt — this small band of Christians offers a balm of healing for profoundly painful wounds.

117

Paul Argiewicz sat in the front row of the synagogue that morning. The sanctuary was filled with emotion — and tension. In keeping with his conviction that his message must be delivered in the German language, Pastor Bittner spoke to the crowd through a translator. His words reflected a contrite and broken heart; his eyes rarely left Paul. At the end of his message, the pastor looked directly at him, then spoke quietly.

"I need to ask for your forgiveness."

The room was silent as Paul stood up and stepped forward. Pastor Jobst walked from behind the *bimah* (Torah podium) and moved toward him. In tears, the two men embraced. The congregation wept, immersed in a moment that will be remembered and cherished by all who witnessed this miracle of forgiveness.

In my American experience — so sheltered from the kind of persecution that made this demonstration of forgiveness so powerful and pure — Paul Argiewicz represents something truly heroic. Having survived the worst that humanity has to offer, he has lived a life exemplifying the best in our nature. He is a true inspiration. My sincere hope is that his story will inspire all of us to become better people. ✡

Paul shares his Holocaust experience with German pastor Jobst Bittner and his translator, Tina Pompe.

Paul and Cheryl's Acknowledgements

In addition to everyone who labored on this book (*see Author's Acknowledgements*), Paul and Cheryl Argiewicz would like to thank the following:

HaShem (G-d) — who watched over me during my darkest hours. All my gratitude to You.

Robert and Lucy Matzner — (Paul's sister and brother-in-law) for all the love, inspiration, and shared memories from childhood. Thank you for helping with the spelling of camp names and for so graciously answering so many questions and phone calls.

Deanne — our love and unending gratitude, without whom this book would have remained only a dream. This was an awesome, incredible labor of love. You have found a permanent place in our hearts and have become our "adopted" daughter. Your family is the icing on the cake.

Donna Lilley (Cheryl's sister) — for your love, support, and encouragement. Thank you especially for holding our hands on our first trip back to the concentration camps and reliving the nightmare with us. (Not to mention shlepping all the luggage!)

Our children — Howard and Susan, Cindy and Steve, Bill and Nathalie, Fred, and Tom and Judy — all of you for unceasing love, hugs, encouragement, and inspiration.

Our grandchildren — our jewels: Heather and Kyllo, Janess, Cody, Jordan, Kyle, Zach, Madie, Max, Heather, Christopher and Heather, Tamara, Noah and Diana, Jaime, Ben and Khava. Our great-grandchildren — who carry on the legacy: Mason, Ella, Sophia, and Noah.

Other survivors — for opening their doors and their hearts to us.

Our dear friends and mentors — for their incredible patience, encouragement, and fortitude: Dr. Werner Linfield, Dr. and Mrs. Irving Kohn, Professor Helene Block-Fields, "Secret Agent" Ed Phelps (who was responsible for Paul's attendance at the lecture where he and Elie Wiesel would meet for the first time — see photo section), Brenda Storm, Irene Carbone, Norma Cox, Nortine Boudghian, Charlene Fieldman, Judi Wepner, Rev. Andy and Bonnie Williams, Rabbi Tzali and Rivkie Wilschanski, Dr. William Becker, Beverly Sorensen, Professor Jesse Scott, and Dr. Howard Lipke.

119

All the principals, professors, teachers, students, and children who honored us by repeatedly inviting us to speak all over the country. Especially Principal Longisto, and teachers Jody Marver, Susan Boudreau, Nancy Daley, Janine Griese, and Judy Morill. Megan Beamon — who came to one of our speeches and wrote a magnificent and touching story. And to the multitude of people who helped and inspired us in so many ways that we couldn't even begin to name . . . hopefully, you know who you are. ✿

Glossary of Terms

Aleph-Bet — the Hebrew alphabet

Aliyah — (Hebrew) literally "to go up" or "ascend"; used in reference to the obtaining of citizenship in Israel

Autobahn — (German) the German superhighway

Baruch HaShem — (Hebrew) a term of praise; literally "Bless the Name" (in reference to God)

Blitzkrieg — (German) "lightning war"

Bruchah — (Hebrew) a blessing

Beurgermeister — German term for the town chairman or mayor

Chuppah — (Hebrew) a traditional canopy under which a bride and groom stand during the wedding ceremony

Crimmitschau — a small town in Saxony, West Germany

Diaspora — the scattering of the Jewish people away from their ancestral homeland

Dirgemeiseh — dehydrated vegetables used in livestock feed

Fuehrer — (German) a leader

Gestapo — the Nazi secret police

Hof an der Saale — (German) a city on the Saale River in Bavaria, West Germany. During the period immediately following the war, it was considered part of the American-occupied territory.

Jude — (German) "Jew"

Judenrein — (German) a land without Jews; lit. "cleansed of Jews"

Kaddishil — (Yiddish) the person who says the blessing for an individual when he or she dies; usually the closest family member

Kapo — a prisoner assigned the task of overseeing and managing other prisoners in the concentration camps

Kehilah — (Hebrew) a religious community or congregation

121

Ketubah — (Hebrew) a legally binding marriage contract

Kipah — (Hebrew) also known as a "yarmulke" in Yiddish; a head covering worn by observant Jews

Kol Nidre — (Hebrew) ancient Aramaic liturgy historically canted on the eve of Yom Kippur; literally, "All Vows"

Kristallnacht — (German) "night of broken glass"

Kukuruza — (Russian) corn

Ma Nishtanah — (Hebrew) a reference to a traditional question asked by Jewish children on the night of Passover: "Why is this night different from all other nights?"

Mazel Tov — (Yiddish) "congratulations" or "good luck"

Mishpucha — (Hebrew/Yiddish) family

Mitzvah — (Hebrew) a "good deed" or obedience to a commandment

Mourner's Kaddish — an ancient Hebrew prayer that is recited or canted at the death (or memorial commemoration of the death) of a loved one.

Olam HaBa — (Hebrew) "the world to come"; the place of compensation for one's deeds after this life

Payot — (Hebrew/Yiddish) an uncut portion of hair on the temples and sideburns—often appearing in locks—and sometimes tucked behind the ear

Pogrom — an organized persecution or massacre of (Jewish) people

Rachmunus — (Hebrew/Yiddish) tender mercy or compassion

Roma — gypsies

Rosh HaShannah — (Hebrew) traditionally accepted as the head of the Jewish new year, its Biblical origin was Yom Teruah, The Day of Blowing (Trumpets)

Schwartzfochs — (pro. sh-VORTZ-fox)

SS — an elite unit within the Nazi party; a special security force

122

Shabbos — (Hebrew/Yiddish) the Jewish Sabbath beginning at sundown, Friday and continuing through sundown, Saturday

Shlep — (Yiddish) to carry or lug

Shmatas — (Yiddish) rags

Shochet — (Hebrew) a man who is trained to butcher animals according to the laws of kashrut (dietary laws of the Bible)

Siddur — a book of liturgical Hebrew prayers and blessings

Succoth — (Hebrew) The Feast of Booths (Tabernacles); an eight day festival during which time the Jewish people are to live in booths, commemorating the forty years they spent in the wilderness after leaving Egypt

Tzadik — (Hebrew) a religious, righteous man; one who keeps the commandments

Tzitzit — (Hebrew) knotted fringes on the corners of garments to remind the children of Israel to keep the commandments of the Torah

Yarmark — an outdoor farmer's market where locals bought and sold goods

Yom Kippur — (Hebrew) The Day of Atonement

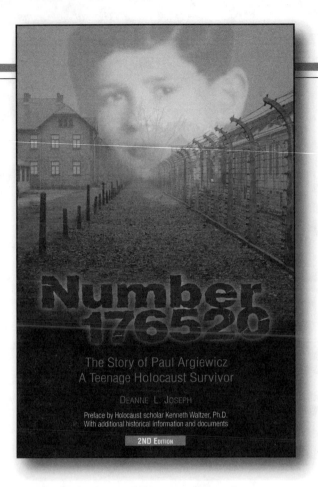

Number 176520
The Story of Paul Argiewicz
A Teenage Holocaust Survivor

DEANNE L. JOSEPH

Preface by Holocaust scholar Kenneth Waltzer, Ph.D.
With additional historical information and documents

2ND EDITION

To purchase additional copies of this book, or for more information on Paul Argiewicz (including scheduling for speaking engagements), contact Blue Thread, Inc:

MAIL
Blue Thread, Inc. ● PO Box 388 ● Salem, WI 53168-0388

PHONE
262-893-5671

E-MAIL / WEB SITE
bluethreadinc@yahoo.com ● www.paulstory.org

Please drop us a line—we'd love to hear from you!